THE SECRETS OF LOST CATS

THE SECRETS OF LOST CATS

One Woman, Twenty Posters, and a New Understanding of Love

DR. NANCY DAVIDSON

St. Martin's Press   New York

This is a work of nonfiction. However, the names of certain individuals and their identifying characteristics have been changed to protect their privacy, and dialogue has been reconstructed to the best of the author's recollection.

THE SECRETS OF LOST CATS. Copyright © 2013 by Dr. Nancy Davidson. All rights reserved. Printed in the United States of America. For information, address St. Martin's Press, 175 Fifth Avenue, New York, N.Y. 10010.

www.stmartins.com

Design by Anna Gorovoy

Library of Congress Cataloging-in-Publication Data

Davidson, Nancy (Nancy L.)
   The secrets of lost cats : one woman, twenty posters, and a new understanding of love / Dr. Nancy Davidson.
      p. cm.
   ISBN 978-1-250-00626-4 (hardcover)
   ISBN 978-1-4668-3532-0 (e-book)
   1. Pet owners—Psychology.   2. Pet loss—Psychological aspects.   3. Human-animal relationships.   4. Davidson, Nancy (Nancy L.)   I. Title.
   SF411.47.D38 2013
   636.80092'9—dc23

                                                           2013009262

St. Martin's Press books may be purchased for educational, business, or promotional use. For information on bulk purchases, please contact Macmillan Corporate and Premium Sales Department at 1-800-221-7945 extension 5442 or write specialmarkets@macmillan.com.

First Edition: July 2013

10 9 8 7 6 5 4 3 2 1

for Shirley Davidson,
who encouraged her children to be curious

CONTENTS

INTRODUCTION 1

ZAK 11

ECCLES 23

WUSS 35

MONTANA MADDY.. 47

NIKO... 65

TORI.. 79

SHELBY.. 93

MAOMY 109

SYDNEY 119

KOOL KAT JELLYBEAN...131

DANGER AND KITTY 141

VANCOUVER JOE 155

BROADWAY LUCY... 165

OLD CAT AND MUFFIN... 175

ZAK, PART TWO 185

MARY... 195

BAILEY... 209

AMSTERDAM SAM 225

SQUEEZER... 235

SPANISH SNOOPY 243

ACKNOWLEDGMENTS... 255

RESOURCES 257

WHAT TO DO WHEN YOUR CAT GOES MISSING... 259

WHAT TO DO WHEN YOU FIND A CAT.................. 263

INTRODUCTION

We've all seen them. Hanging on telephone poles, mailboxes, and posted on the bulletin boards of our local supermarkets. LOST! REWARD! HAVE YOU SEEN JOEY? The blaring headlines of the lost-cat poster call to us, as does the picture of Joey stretched out asleep on the living room rug, vulnerable belly exposed, feet suspended in the air. The caption underneath the picture offers a sliver of information yet somehow says it all: *Friendly. Loud meower. Likes treats. Owner heartbroken.* Most of us feel pangs for the missing cat and the distraught owner. Where could Joey be? Is he hiding or lost? Is he hurt or sick?

A lost-cat poster tells the beginning of a story. But only the beginning. Most of us—at least those of us who love animals and mysteries—want to know more. We have a desire to fill in the blanks, a need to understand a story that is, to us, unknown. What happened? Why did Joey vanish? Will the missing cat and the anxious owner reunite? Will there be a happy ending? Although our questions are rarely—if ever—answered, the public's role in the unfolding drama is anything but a mystery. Frantic cat owners rely upon hundreds and possibly thousands of deputy searchers to be on the lookout for their missing kitty, phoning in possible sightings or tips. We become part of the rescue team. We become detectives.

A lost-cat poster is, in effect, an invitation to care about a missing loved one. Our busy, task-filled day has been interrupted by a stranger's vulnerability. Love has gone missing.

I've been on both sides of a lost-cat poster. I know firsthand all the feelings an owner pours into making one. When my cat, Zak, disappeared, I had to make my very own poster. I was desperate. I searched for my orange tabby everywhere: schoolyards, side streets, parked cars, garbage cans. Rambling through a neighbor's yard on one moonless night, I accidentally tripped their security system and found myself blinded by floodlights while a very large and upset homeowner ran toward me.

"I'm only looking for my cat. *Honest!*" I explain.

At the time, I was living in New Haven, Connecticut, a small city filled with nineteenth-century houses clustered around Yale University's sprawling campus. I worked at home as a psychotherapist and Zak, my big orange tabby, spent a lot of time with me during the day. He liked to go hunting after hours, but I could always count on him to come home during the late-night talk shows, or at least by infomercial time. But one fateful night he never showed up, and he forgot all about breakfast—which was sacred to us.

He'll come home soon, I told myself. *He'll come trotting in with a mouse that he'll drop proudly at my feet.*

The day wasted away and by evening, I stalked the neighborhood with my flashlight. When midnight hit, I was sitting on the porch, waiting, hoping that silence, patience, and a steady gaze at the sidewalk would prove more effective. Eventually I went to bed, but sleep was ragged. I strained to hear Zak's signal—one paw banging against my bedroom window.

I wondered if I was to blame. Maybe I'd given Zak too much freedom? Or maybe my love wasn't enough and he'd found a better deal somewhere else? My rational self disagreed. "Where could he get a better deal? I feed him real albacore tuna!"

The next morning, I had to accept the truth. Zak was missing. His disappearance was officially an emergency. A breath crawled out of my tight chest. So many thoughts and feelings erupted.

Helpless: *This can't be true.*

Overwhelmed: *Where do I start?*

Fear: *I don't want to feel this pain.*

Doom: *Will I ever see my sweet boy again?*

One loss has a way of reactivating the memories of other losses. I felt the past creeping up, with the memory of lost loved ones. I refused to revisit this excruciating feeling of abandonment. I had to fight it. I had to find Zak.

This time I had a chance—maybe I could find the one I loved. I drew in a deeper breath. Zak was smart, and he'd only been missing a day. I still had a chance to find him. I raced into my office and drew up several prototypes of lost-cat posters. I didn't know which words to use. "HELP!" summarized my need, but its message seemed vague. "I'm a mess" would be accurate, but not strategic. I felt frustrated, but I tried to hurry. Zak disappeared before smartphones and instant photographs were ubiquitous. Instead I drew a picture of him, with a hint of a smile. He was a happy cat. I experimented with the captions: "Missing Cat," "Last Seen"—before finally settling on the true simplicity of our situation—*LOST.* Zak and me.

I went out on the street carrying a stack of posters. As I hammered, people stopped to offer sympathy. "I hope you find your kitty," one lady said. A couple walking by offered, "Good luck," and "You'll find him." After I had put up the posters—I started with twenty—I went home. I slouched in a chair by the phone, and waited for the world—or some divinity—to intervene. An hour later, I was back on the street. Active anxiety seemed more heroic than waiting.

The next day, while I was out searching, an earnest young man called and left a message:

"My wife and I saw an orange tabby that looked like yours, around midnight, two days ago, in the garden by the Polish church on State Street. I couldn't get close because he was wild and snarly. I hope this helps. Good luck!"

Was it helpful? Let's see. Over forty-eight hours ago they saw a deranged, orange cat at midnight in the garden of good and evil. Honestly, it wasn't what I wanted to hear, and there was no return phone number. Nevertheless, I hurried over to trespass on the church grounds, afraid that my sweet kitty, who usually said hello by licking my nose, had been transformed into a feral vampire cat. While searching the churchyard, I stopped to gaze at a ten-foot-tall statue of Saint-I-Have-No-Idea and suddenly thought: *Zak is a lapsed Jew with Buddhist tendencies. He is so not here.*

On the walk home I began to wonder about other cat owners. Were they able to laugh at themselves like I was? And how did they end up finding their cats? I was thankful that, as a psychotherapist in private practice, I had a flexible work schedule, but what about cat owners who punched a clock? Instead of searching for their missing cats, they were trapped at work. Were friends and relatives helping them?

How many empathetic phone calls did they get? I had received about fifteen—strangers, each and every one of them—from people who wished me good luck, even though they didn't have any information to pass along. Each time I hit the playback button, I decided that *this* would be the one pinpointing Zak's location.

When I finally arrived home, the house felt empty and lonely. Tears rolled down my face. I couldn't think about other cat owners. I had to find *my* cat.

Searching for Zak changed my life. I became acutely and permanently aware of lost-cat posters. I saw them everywhere—in my hometown, on the streets surrounding my office in Manhattan, all across the country, even on vacation in Europe. They were on lampposts, in my local deli, at the post office, and on gas station walls. One was even tacked onto a tree outside my living room window.

I lingered in front of them, studying their composition. All of them made me feel empathic, but some posters made me smile, too. A photograph captured the image of a tiny kitten being groomed by her mother's tongue. One man drew a picture of a black cat and wrote, "We love him." I discovered twins. Two brothers both had similar dark markings around their eyes; named respectively, the Lone Ranger and Tonto.

One day, I impulsively took a poster home—it had a picture of a red Abyssinian named Lilly. Soon, there was no denying it. I was out and out collecting lost-cat posters (I'd make sure there were duplicates posted nearby, or I'd Xerox one in a nearby copy shop and put the original back where I found it). In part, I was drawn to their folk art quality, but mostly I was intrigued by the messages themselves. I wondered why some owners included extraneous information. It made sense to list the cat's color or personality traits or home address, but the cat's birthday? What were we supposed to do? Send a card?

Eventually, it occurred to me that each owner—knowingly or unknowingly—felt compelled to tell a story.

Family heartbroken . . .

Owner desperate . . .

Cat needs medication . . .

Other cats miss him . . .

Some posters looked like they came right out of the family photo album. You could see young kids in the pictures. A kitchen table. Others seemed put together in great haste. Some were accompanied by beautiful drawings; others were text only. A few read like poems.

Gradually, my desire to collect lost-cat posters came into focus.

I wanted to find out about the cats but I also wanted to know who the cats were leaving behind. The posters became a portal into the subculture of lost-cat owners; the phone numbers the entry point and the means to pass through. I'd call and introduce myself, ask a few questions, empathize, and say, "Thank you." I'd be an armchair Nancy Drew with a specialty, I mulled over my title—"Lost-Cat Detective," or possibly "Cat-Poster Sleuth."

But when it came to making the first phone call, Nancy Drew's confidence wavered. The last thing I wanted to do was give someone false hope. What if the owner felt intruded upon? Feeling shy, I dialed the number on Lilly's poster. A young woman answered the phone. I introduced myself by saying, "I'm a cat lover who writes about lost and found cats and I hope you . . ." but she cut me off mid-sentence.

"Oh, it's such a *bizarre* story," she said, bursting with enthusiasm.

In those halcyon days at the beginning of my journey, it really was that simple. Most of the stories that I heard were hilarious—even the melancholy ones had their moments of lightness. But as my collection grew, the stories became more complex, and sometimes sadly dark. Lost-cat owners seemed to be like protagonists trapped inside a film noir. Left to rely on dead-end clues, intuition, and guts, how could they escape? Nancy Drew tugged on her fedora.

I realized that cats could vanish innocently or as a result of malice. The animal's character, personality, and temperament influenced the nature of an owner's search—the when, the where, and the how long. My curiosity exploded. Owners were under constant pressure to make the right decision. *Should they exercise caution or take a risk*? "I searched in an area where drug dealers hang out." *Stay patient or be impulsive?* "I was so happy to see my cat that I ran toward her, but she got scared and ran into the woods."

Conversations with the cat owners and my clients seemed strikingly similar. Although I didn't introduce myself as a therapist, I was startled when owners asked me for advice. ("Do you believe in dreams?") Some of my friends wanted to know if I was doing pro bono therapy. I didn't know what to tell them. The doctor in me couldn't help but notice that talking with owners about their missing (and even found) cats was ultimately a conversation about the loss of control. ("I don't know whether to get my daughter a new kitten, or hold out for Lilly's return." "Even if your gut tells you it's not your cat, how can you *not* leave work, *not* go check out a lead?" "If I stop looking, it's like admitting he's dead." "No one cares, except me.")

The process of searching for a lost cat and the process of therapy can be likened to an odyssey. By definition, an odyssey is filled with darkness, confusion, and obstacles, where turning back is no longer an option. In order to move forward, we must summon bravery, determination, inventiveness, resilience, faith, and forgiveness. Hope matters deeply. At the end of the journey, we see the world—and ourselves—differently.

We may discover that there are many types of happy endings. One cat owner said, "I lost my cat, but gained a community," and I observed my clients addressing similar journeys in their lives—without having lost their cats. ("I lost my dad, but I met all the people he was closest to.")

For seven years, I followed where my curiosity led me. I'd unintentionally discovered—like any heroine searching for something outside of her sunlit and shadowed self—an unfinished epic of my own. At the end of my odyssey I felt changed as a human being, a cat owner, a family member, and a psychotherapist. As Rilke said, "Be patient toward all that is unsolved in your heart and try to love the questions themselves."

There is a question about love that grips most of us—animal lovers or not. We react to it constantly, although not always consciously. When we become aware of its presence we typically feel passionate, if not conflicted, about how well we're answering the question in our own lives. It's haunting us, always slumbering in our consciousness, never leaving our hearts, ever present in therapy.

What would you do for love?

Some of us begin by making a lost-cat poster.

ZAK

Five days after Zak's disappearance, I'd learned nothing as to his whereabouts. People had called to wish me luck—but no one in the neighborhood had seen Zak. Not even Old Man Tony, who sat on his porch steps every day overseeing the comings and goings on the street. Eddie didn't know, either. Eddie was the developmentally disabled man who lived with his mother across the street. Middle-aged but spry, he used to put Zak in his bicycle basket and ride with him around the block. Zak liked it, but after I saw Eddie pedaling away from our street with my cat at the helm, I had to stop the carnival ride.

I knew that my best hope for finding Zak rested on the foot-traffic flow of strangers who may or may not stop to read my lost-cat poster, my own plea for help. But what were the statistics on finding your missing cat? I had no idea, but I wanted to give Zak the best possible odds. So when I searched for him—and I searched every day—I carried extra posters and a staple gun. A previously unexplored street would soon have a set of posters with Zak's handsome face tacked to streetlights—on each side of the street. I wasn't leaving anything to chance.

During my search, I quickly discovered my psychological borders—what I considered my emotional-neighborhood turf.

We all have these emotional maps, whether we realize it or not. We'll go to this convenience store, not that one. We'll buy our coffee here, not there. We won't cross at these lights, preferring instead the block ahead. It's simple, really. We feel more comfortable in some places than others. Surely that must be true for animals, too. I thought about that as I continued to search for Zak. If he has to be missing, I reasoned, then at least let me find him on a street that felt soothing, a friendly looking street. As crazy as it sounds, I wanted Zak to feel comforted. Maybe on a nice street he'd feel less lonely.

Yes, I anthropomorphized that Zak had human feelings—mine. I knew the difference between his core animal needs and my human ones, but intellect couldn't stop my worries. I wished I could send a message through mental telepathy. At least he'd know that I was frantically looking for him.

After five days of searching I understood the importance of the elements. Rain, in particular, posed a threat. Besides worrying that my posters would disintegrate, I worried that Zak was wet and cold. It had rained that morning, so I was out checking the telephone poles to see which posters had survived. Some were perfectly intact, while others were left dangling by a staple. A few had been so ravaged that Zak's likeness resembled an Impressionist painting gone soggy.

I had to get to work. The sun pushing through the clouds meant that people would soon be traveling on the sidewalks, and perhaps stopping to read my posters—a crayon drawing of an orange cat. SOS.

Nothing worked. The hours drummed by; days and nights passed of not knowing. Dread walked with me. Five days after his disappearance, I gave in. I picked up the phone.

"Hello, do you find lost pets? Could I hire you? My cat is missing."

I heard silence, followed by the click of a lighter and a long, breathy inhalation of smoke. Then the deep, raspy voice of an elderly woman who'd obviously downed some gin in her day replied: *"He's alive!"* She exhaled.

My nightmare was over?

"Really! Really? How do you know?" I was feeling the surge of relief, but I wasn't going to be totally taken in. I had my suspicions.

"He's a beautiful, big cat . . . orange." She took another drag from her cigarette. "Bushy tail." *How did she get his coloring right? How did she know that he was handsome?* Pride swooped in. Zak was *alive* and still good looking.

"He's been gone five days," I said.

"There's a neighborhood kid." Exhale. "A young boy. He knows."

My heart sank. "The strange kid next door," I said. "But they're away. Nobody's seen them for days."

"Very friendly, handsome."

"Yeah, that's Zaky. Did the boy do something to him?"

"The little boy knows."

"Is there something else I should know?"

"The boy knows." Inhale.

"Okay, okay. What do I owe you?"

"Nothing."

Click.

I'd made the call after my vision cleared. I'd been at my desk crying when I saw the psychic's card lying on top of Zak's posters. I had to decide whether contacting the psychic was brilliant or insane. Brilliant meant that I had faith in my ability to think outside the box. Insane meant that I was desperate to believe in magic. It also made me vulnerable to a con job. It's not that I'm against creative solutions, but in this case it was the source of the suggestion—a client—who gave me pause.

Zak had been my sometimes co-therapist for ten years. I didn't encourage him to enter the field. He chose it himself. When he was a kitten, I spent as much quality time with him as

I could, but when it was time to work, I closed my office door. Not one to be put off so easily he'd wander down the hall, sit right outside my door, and meow. A lot. I'd see his little paws under the crack of the door, but I never stopped the session, knowing he'd fall asleep soon enough. Until one day, at the end of a particularly intense exchange, a client burst into laughter. I followed her eyes and saw two little orange front paws—pad sides up—sticking out from under the office door. Apparently, Zak had fallen asleep on his back. And resting on the floor, in between his paws, were two upside down orange ear tips. "Can he come in?" my client asked.

He was a great therapy cat; even the cat-hating curmudgeons all thought Zak was "cool." They especially appreciated the way he'd escort them to their sessions. Springing onto the hood of a parked car, he would walk across the front windshield and stare at the driver with his big yellow eyes. He'd wait until the client opened the driver's side door and then accompany him or her up the porch stairs and into my home office. Then they'd both sit down—the client on the couch and Zak on the rug. Some of my shy clients would use Zak's presence as a conversational starting point to share how their childhood pets had saved them from feeling lonely. After one woman revealed that she couldn't trim her cat's nails, we had a touching session about the pervasive sense of inadequacy she carried with her. She counted her inability to carry out this task (a task that challenges a lot of cat owners), as just one more personal failing. And then there was the time when, over the course of one session, a young woman sobbed so deeply that she lost her breath and started to choke. Zak's ears went back. He made a high-pitched *meow* and jumped into her lap, covering her stomach with his body. Her breathing softened and she began to pet him. She smiled and said, "He's trying to help."

But after Zak disappeared, as each client arrived for his or her appointment, they'd ask, "Where's the cat?" I kept my cool at first, but eventually I'd stopped answering the question. I'd simply wave my lost-cat poster in the air, like it was my turn for show and tell.

Kate was the client who'd suggested that I call her psychic. An intelligent woman with a lot going for her, she was not, within the context of our therapy sessions, what I'd refer to as a "hard worker." Kate almost always took the easy way out, and when she didn't agree with what I had to say, she went to a psychic for a second opinion. I declined when she offered me her psychic's services, but at the end of the session, on her way out, she dropped the card on my desk anyway. I had no intention of calling, but a hard cry had washed away my resistance and I was willing to try anything. Besides I needed help, and the psychic's credibility had skyrocketed after I learned that we agreed on one fundamental truth—Kate's affair would break up her marriage. I dialed.

The psychic's promise—"He's alive!"—was still my only clue, and my new neighbors had been identified as material witnesses. They'd been gone for exactly *five* days. Zak had been missing exactly *five* days. Coincidence was on my side. So were my instincts. I never had a great feeling about these neighbors. The husband bulked up on steroids, but despite mountains of muscle he seemed incapable of pushing a lawn mower across his scrawny city yard. His wife chain-smoked and screamed at the kids. Even their son was suspect after he had impulsively chopped down—in my own yard—a small green tree.

"It was ugly," he told me.

Finding my cat had become a moral imperative. Now that the psychic had given me hope, I hatched a plan. Since there were probably clues inside the neighbors' house that would lead me to Zak, I'd wait until dark and break in. My role model, Nancy Drew, would have asked one of her chums to be the lookout, so I asked my friend Susan to help. When she said, "Yes," I assumed that she understood I was the lead detective and she was the chum. Chums follow their leader. But when the evening stars began to glow, Susan became anxious. She wanted to call the police and inform them of our plans, just to be on the safe side.

"Tell them what?" I asked. "We're planning a break-in?"

While we sat on the back stairs of the neighbor's house arguing, a sweet black cat with a bell on his collar appeared and climbed into my lap. It had to be a sign. Our mission had been blessed, but Susan couldn't shake her desire to call the cops. She went to get the cordless phone while the black kitty and I waited. Twenty minutes passed.

Finally, Susan returned, carrying the phone. The police dispatcher had put her on hold because her supervisor needed to be notified. My sarcasm trickled out. "The police might be looking up the rules on future break-in protocol, *or* they might be desperately wishing you'd hang up because it's hard for them to write up a report about a crime that hasn't happened yet." Susan laughed, but her conscience waited it out on the phone.

"You're killing the Nancy Drew thing," I growled. "The whole point is we're *sneaking* in." The black kitty trotted off.

After a few more minutes, my patience followed suit.

"Just hang up," I said. "They don't have our address, right?" Susan didn't respond. "Perfect. You called in a future felony, gave them our address, stayed on the phone hoping to get a message from the supervisor. 'We're making an exception, 'cause you girls are so honest. In fact, we applaud the noble rescue of a cat by two respectable women with no criminal record. Break the law and have a nice day!' Look, they're freaking out. They'd prefer we zip it and not talk into their tape-recorded phone log. I'm going in, with or without you."

Susan put the phone down and followed me up the stairs to the neighbor's second-floor deck. "You are the lookout person," I told her. "Lean over the railings and scan the street for the neighbors, possible witnesses, and, let me add, a police cruiser."

I sized up the bedroom windows. Which one would be the easi-
est to break? I had to get inside . . . though I don't know what I
was expecting to find. One lame lead from a chain-smoking
psychic and I had the energy of a mother lifting a piano to rescue her child. I shouted Zak's name and pointed my flashlight
into the darkness behind the sliding glass doors. While jiggling
the lock I continued to press my face up against the glass, but it
was hard to make anything out. Then, for a fraction of a second,
in a corner of the jet-black room . . . a blur of orange.

Was I hallucinating? Was this some sort of apparition?

"Zaky! Zaky?"

Out of the darkness he strolled, as if in slow motion, toward
the light. I crouched down and placed my palm on the sliding
glass window. It was like a prison visit. His orange body rubbed
up against the glass where my hand pressed from the visitor's
side. "I'm gonna get you out!" I shouted. I saw his mouth move,
but his little meow was silenced by the barrier between us.
"Hold on butterscotch baby boy," I yelled at the glass.

Susan was equally thunderstruck at the sight of Zak. Here he
was stuck in an abandoned house, without food or water, in the
suffocating August heat. What if he was sick? We were morally
outraged and highly motivated, but we'd forgotten the part
where you bring actual burglary tools. Recovering from that
tactical lapse, I summoned up my anger and smashed the cellar
window with my flashlight. Susan slithered through the creepy
spiderweb-covered basement and ran up to the second floor.
Then she carried Zak down and, reaching through the window,
placed him in my arms.

I wish I could say that Zak licked my face and snuggled like a
bunny, but no, he just squirmed about in my arms. He liked his
newfound freedom and didn't appreciate my smothering of affection, so I let him jump down and the three of us stumbled
down the neighbor's unpaved driveway.

I kicked a stone and tried to make sense of what had happened.

A psychic had said that Zak was alive and the boy next door knew something. But he'd disappeared five days ago, just like Zak. From that tip, I intuited that there would be some type of information in the house that would help me find Zak, and ignored any hesitation that I may have had about breaking in. My cat needed me more than social convention needed another minion.

In my kitchen, Zak devoured a freedom-celebration tuna dinner but then made his way toward the front door, as if he'd lost all memory of his incarceration. Susan and I followed him outside. He rubbed up against our legs and meowed. He sat on the porch stairs with us. Then we decided we should cover our crime of passion. We tacked a board over the neighbor's broken window and wiped off our fingerprints. The cops never showed up.

Susan worried that the neighbors would eventually see the lost-cat posters and then it would be apparent that we were the ones who had rescued Zak so she ripped down all of the posters. Afterward I told her the poster wouldn't send us to the Big House. "What are they going to do? Call the cops, and say, 'The cat we kidnapped is missing?'"

But this wouldn't be the last chapter—eventually the neighbors would return. I needed a strategy and a personal checkup, so I summoned my inner therapist. Were the neighbors the type to retaliate? You can never be sure, but I didn't think so. They drank a lot, but I'd never seen them hit their children or even heard them fight as a couple. Mainly, they seemed irresponsible and immature but I was mad, a little scared, and feeling resentful. I didn't want to live next to them, even if they *were* nonviolent. After they returned, what would life be like for Zak, if I let him outside? What if the boy had an obsession with Zak? I knew I had to speak with his parents.

A week later, the neighbors pulled into their driveway and began unpacking the car. I gritted my teeth and said hello from the front porch. Zak was napping on the sidewalk in front of their house. I went over to him and suggested that he sleep in front of *our* house, but he clearly wanted to gloat about his get-out-of-jail-free card. No one said a negative word. In fact, the father and son were friendly. I looked for signs of distress in their presentation. I watched the boy dart around the front yard doing nothing in particular, but talking incessantly, mostly uttering fantastic stories. When he went over to pet Zak he lost his balance. It was then that I realized he had motor-coordination problems. If I hadn't been so annoyed with him for cutting down my tree, I would have put it together sooner—he had attention deficit disorder with hyperactivity. His symptoms were in motion: excessive talking, impulsivity, frustration, and distractibility. Forgetfulness is another key symptom of ADHD. I'll bet that he took Zak inside the house and simply forgot about him. Then the parents locked the doors and the family went on vacation.

It was only a theory, but it was win-win. Zak would be safe, and I no longer had to fret about my neighbors or worry about the boy.

But days later, the ordeal continued to replay itself over and over in my head. I saw Zak trapped behind the glass. I saw myself breaking the window. What if I hadn't called the psychic? Maybe I'd never have found Zak. What if I hadn't broken in but, instead, discovered much later that he'd been locked inside all along? I would never have been able to forgive myself. How did I feel about the risks I took? I loved him so much that if I got into trouble, I'd live with the consequences.

A month later, the fury and drama had ebbed. Routines were resumed. While walking around the neighborhood, stop and start became the new norm; at telephone poles I skimmed past the posters for rock bands, tag sales, volunteers needed, and computer help. I was looking for lost-cat posters. I found them, too.

Vary wary Middie, may be hiding.

Spidey is black and has three legs. Gets around well.

A cat named Itchy had a brother named Ritchie who wasn't missing.

The experience with Zak had triggered something in me. I wanted to pass along the support that I'd been surprised to receive, mostly from strangers, who'd left messages of concern after discovering Zak's posters. Those calls—so many from people I didn't know and would never meet—had left me feeling a little more hopeful, a little less alone. Most of us have asked ourselves, more than once: *Who will be there for me? Who cares about my problems? Will loved ones and strangers help me or will they add to my troubles?* When our pets disappear we feel scared. For other lost-cat owners I wanted to offer my tiny flame of goodness for their foggy trek.

People were friendly, but surprised to hear from me. "What's your name again?"

I discovered a black-and-white sketch of a cat, which had a big head, spots on his nose, and a bouncy tail. The caption said, *Of course, in person he looks more like a cat.* The father of the owner, an elderly Italian man had learned more nouns than verbs. "Thunder, boom, lightning, she a gone," he said, referring to their twenty-two-year-old cat who had run away. "Neighbor lady find, laundry basket."

Then one day I discovered a poster that included a figure of a heart, with an arrow drawn through it. The owner told me a very long, haunting story. She'd been on a journey. Like the devoted wife of a sea captain who would climb the stairs to the widow walk—at dawn and at dusk—she would scan the horizon searching for a hint of a tiny ship in the distance, her gaze exuding a prayer and a question: *When is he coming home?*

<u>REWARD</u>

"Eccles" <u>CAT</u> missing since
8/22
Large Gray + White Male
East Rock Park + Vicinity.

He has a shaved underbelly.
May have lost Collar + Name
Tag.

<u>Please Help</u> - Owner is
♡ Broken

(203) 555-8237
(203) 555 1432

ECCLES

REWARD topped the page, but EMERGENCY would have been more accurate. Black on white, handwritten, and easily duplicated, this was a hastily produced poster. "Eccles" took the lead in the opening sentence, followed by a qualifier, "cat." The explanation was welcome, because I had no idea what an "Eccles" was. Apparently, the owner had started writing her poster without realizing that the public would need some basic facts. For starters, Eccles was a cat.

According to the poster, Eccles had a shaved underbelly, which implied a recent visit to the vet. Sick and missing, no wonder the owner was in a hurry to find her boy. Two phone numbers were scribbled below a pair of declarations, "Please Help!" and "Owner is heartbroken!" The latter phrase had the word "heart" substituted with a drawing of one. Males are genetically loath to draw a picture of a heart, never mind hanging one on a tree for public display. That was my first clue in identifying the owner. Without a doubt, a young woman was desperate to find Eccles.

"I saw him emerge from the bushes in East Rock," Holly told me when I called, referring to a park in New Haven. "Although he didn't notice me. The regular joggers had named him 'Rocky.' According to them, he was a big, tough guy with muscular legs. But I thought he looked sweet and handsome, with his gray-and-white markings," she said. I smiled. Bad Boy Rocky, leader of the pack. *Vroom!*

"I'd put food and water in bowls on the ground and then leave," Holly said. "He needed the space." Weeks later, Rocky still dined alone, but as long as Holly remained a significant distance from his food bowl, he tolerated her presence. "Each time I saw him, I put my hand out just a little bit. I didn't want to frighten him."

Their relationship reached a new level of intimacy when he stopped hissing at her. Soon thereafter, he no longer backed up when she approached, although his tail remained arched. Finally his ears relaxed. The stare was the last to go. It was progress, but Holly yearned for something more physical. Still, she knew enough not to force herself on him. It was Rocky who took the next step. One day, she reached out her hand, and just like that, he rubbed up against it. She was thrilled.

It was a long-distance relationship, albeit one that was making slow progress, but apparently Holly had to do all the traveling. Rocky hadn't even noticed her at first. Now it seemed that Holly was all give and Rocky was all take. The therapist in me had seen this couple before.

For over twenty-five years, I've helped individuals, couples, and groups, but couples therapy is my specialty, and in times of need, I'm handy with a scientific study. For example, I've learned that researchers at the Gottman Institute in Seattle, Washington, are able to predict with about 90 percent accuracy whether or not a couple engaged in therapy will—three to six years later—remain together or divorce. How can they achieve such accuracy? They videotape the couple during a session. Afterward they watch the tape without the sound and simply observe the couple's body language. Are the partners receptive to each other or not? Does their body language appear conciliatory or does it show a stalemate? Without words to distract them, the researchers are able to discern a couple's response to each other and, therefore, make a much more accurate prediction. Words do play a part, though, and the researchers found that predicting a couple's future together rested on their individual responses to a few salient questions, one of which explores the beginning of their relationship: "What attracted you to your spouse?"

I ask that question in my own practice. With their partners sitting right next to them, people will answer the question eagerly. ("He wasn't like my ex-husband." "She seemed grateful for my help." "I didn't like him at first, but he grew on me." "She was opinionated, but I didn't mind.") I know that a relationship is troubled when a spouse answers by bringing up the negativities that he or she overlooked at the beginning of the courtship. Obviously there were positive things that brought the two of them together, so bringing up only the negative indicates that the marriage is in serious trouble of coming apart.

Positive answers about the past offer something to build upon. ("He was cute and smart." "I knew on the first date that she's the one." "He makes me laugh." "She was honest, no games.") Positive partners may smile or make meaningful eye contact with each other while answering the question. Granted, women tend to be more verbal, but it's the degree of warmth or negativity from either gender that indicates whether the relationship is on stable ground.

Perhaps I shouldn't have been using statistics to prop up my suspicions over Rocky's disappearance, but I was concerned. If Rocky joined the conversation, I was afraid he might say, "She comes over to my place. She cooks and cleans. What's not to like?"

As Holly continued her story, it became clear to me that—like the beginning of so many relationships—a crisis had brought them together. Rocky had the freedom of a stray. He could explore and hunt whenever he wanted to, but he faced the danger that came along with it. The roads in East Rock are inviting, but they're narrow and filled with blind curves, and drivers like to speed. Months after Holly began courting Rocky she found him lying immobile on the side of the road. "I thought maybe he'd been the victim of a hit-and-run," she said. "I went back to my house, grabbed a cat carrier, and drove over to rescue him. The vet couldn't tell me how he'd been hurt, but he was too ill to be on his own." And so Nurse Holly took him home.

That's when she dropped the new name on him. Apparently she'd been saving "Eccles" for a new cat. Maybe Rocky wished she'd saved it for a rainy day instead. The name came to her earlier that year, in a PBS special—a documentary filmed in England—about science and how it's taught in elementary schools. In one segment, students studying the food chain go to a farm. On their field trip, they observe a crowd of cats chasing mice around the barn. One cat in particular is clearly a born hunter, and when he shows up with yet another mouse in his paws, the narrator announces, in a crisp British accent, "Eccles, Eccles again!" I remained silent. Holly laughed and said, "You had to be there.

"When I first got the cat he stayed with me through a tough stretch," she explained, referring to a period of depression following college. "We hung out in the house together. I read a lot and he sat with me while I pondered the 'What-do-I-do-with-my-life?' question. He'd go outside, but he always came back. Somehow he knew it wasn't the time to wander."

I could hear the gratitude in her voice and picture the two of them sitting together, their body language signifying companionship and comfort. Contentment. All is right with the world, I have a good book and my handsome kitty for company. Did

Eccles know that she needed him? Was it true or a result of her magical thinking? Intuition? Unseen forces? It doesn't matter. Holly was telling me about *her* bond with Eccles.

After the depression lifted, Eccles would stay away for days, sometimes even weeks, and Holly would make a perfunctory visit to the shelters to cover all her bases. But the real hunt always began back in East Rock Park. It was the first place Holly went to hang up a lost-cat poster, and every time Eccles disappeared, someone who'd seen the poster would call her. Eccles and Holly would reunite, and rejoice, and Eccles would stop wandering for a while. He'd live the life of a domestic cat until it seemed his memory chip failed and his default setting went into activation: *stray cat.*

I found it easy to feel affection for Eccles. He had the exploratory instincts of a semi-feral cat but he seemed attached to Holly when he was with her. His behavior was less chaotic than the words "ran away" suggested. A better explanation would be that he "faded away." Lingering and napping, roaming for an hour or two, gliding into the afternoon, then completely gone.

I also admired Holly's ability to live with uncertainty. She was sturdy; not too many people choose to stay empathic while dealing with a dicey love. When Eccles returned, there wouldn't be the satisfaction of a screaming match or the pleasure of making up. All she could do is scoop him into her arms, say, "Kitty, kitty, you're home," and hope that he wouldn't do it again.

I understood Holly's predicament. In fact, I felt a lot of empathy for her, but her story was made for self-help: "Women Who Love Cats Who Leave Them." It was a short-lived joke because, satire aside, she was just like the thousands of animal lovers who rescue strays every day.

I wasn't so different from Holly. I'd once had a Creamsicle-colored cat I had named "Sam the Stray." We kept company for about two years. He came and went on his own for days at a time. He often slept in the gutter outside the window of the second-floor apartment in my building. It seemed like a meta-phor for his ambitions in life. But I understood my role—I was one of many boxcar stops for that little hobo.

If we're honest, we know the savior lives within all of us. Rescue the downtrodden, teach them to love, and turn them into an ideal partner or pet. Holly's love for Eccles personified all that was fragile and one-sided about loving a stray. Their life together rested on her hope, and the subsequent actions she took to find him.

It was only a short leap from Holly to understanding how my clients ended up in therapy, rationalizing the misdeeds of their loved ones. ("He's not a bad person, just hotheaded." "He's really sorry." "You don't know him like I do." "He had a tough past." "She says she wants to change." "She's really vulnerable, she just doesn't show it.")

(I'm well-versed in these excuses, and not just because I've conducted several decades of couples counseling. Full disclosure—I've been a sap, too.)

Holly was unusually tenacious, but Eccles eventually pushed the limits of her capacity to cope with uncertainty and she hit rock bottom. In addition to her usual search protocol, Holly placed an ad in the classifieds and called Public Works in New Haven to ask if any dead or injured cats had been reported. She'd been confident in the past that, given enough time, she would find Eccles. But earlier that year, she'd scheduled two months of vacation in Europe, and instead of feeling excited, she felt anxious. "How would Eccles come home," she asked, "if I wasn't there?" As her flight drew near, she resigned herself to his disappearance. "I was glad that I got to love him," she said.

While she was traveling, her answering machine sat at home, blinking in the dark. Two months later, Holly finally replayed the message.

"A young woman saw my poster tacked on the bulletin board in Claire's Café," Holly told me, electrified. "And she also read the board on the opposite wall. It had a cat poster, but it was for a *found* cat. The descriptions seemed similar so she went out of her way to call me. That was really thoughtful."

The creator of the *found* poster was a graduate student living in an apartment downtown. He found Eccles just outside of the park, drifting about and looking hungry. Eccles had been his guest for an entire month, but he wasn't checked in under his own name. Once again, the gray-and-white cat was named after some real or imagined association, or maybe the current identity of the guardian. The newest persona projected onto this beautiful boy must have been that of an academic. Otherwise, how do you can account for the name Bernard?

"Rocky made some sense," Holly said. Then, taking a jab at herself, she added, "Maybe Eccles was a stretch. But Bernard? Who names a cat Bernard?"

So Eccles came home, and it was for Holly as if the breeze through her window had returned with him. She was afloat for several months, until Eccles became ill. It was swift. "I took him to the vet for some tests," she said. "They shaved his belly and sedated him." Her voice thickened. "We drove home and I opened the passenger side door to let him out, and in an instant he took off. He jumped out of his carrier and out the window. I don't know if he was disoriented after waking up from the sedation, but I ran after him, and he disappeared."

Considering the disruptive circumstances and the medical poking at the vet's, it's understandable that Eccles, who was already not feeling well, got angry. At the very least his flight-or-fight limbic brain took over. In humans, the limbic brain is our primitive part that makes us impulsive, instinctual, and easily upset. But people can use another part of their brain, the prefrontal cortex, and apply rational thoughts to manage intense emotion. Without a prefrontal cortex, cats, as far as we know, have only their instincts to protect them.

By the time I saw his lost-cat poster, Eccles had been missing for three months, and his shaved underbelly must have grown in. "Eccles never found his way back on his own." Holly added, firmly. "Humans always found him."

That was good news. People were responding to her lost-cat posters, but I was surprised about Eccles. After a few years of living together there should have been more equanimity to his comings and goings. I'd lulled myself into believing that Eccles occasionally volunteered, like a decent fella, to come home, at least for a few weeks at a time. Instead, every reunion came about because of Holly's hard work. Maybe Eccles had another owner on the other side of town, someone else who was feeding him.

But too many months had passed without an Eccles sighting and Holly sensed that Eccles was gone for good this time. She didn't whitewash the situation. "Maybe Eccles strayed too far," she said. "Maybe he was sick, or died, or somebody kept him. Of course, I'm *hoping* somebody kept him."

She told me that she'd cried the other day for the first time. "Crying means he's not coming back," she said. It was almost as if an oracle within had spoken and released her. She embraced the current truth. And despite their extraordinary number of reunions, Holly wasn't in the throes of romantic blindness. Maybe having been present, at last, during his literal call to the wild, she was saved from blaming herself or worrying that she had the power to change him.

After we spoke, I remained saddened by Holly's loss. With other owners who hadn't recovered their missing cats, I'd felt sad in the moment, but there was something in particular about Holly's longing that haunted me. At the time, other than attributing it to her monumental efforts to find him, I didn't know why. I couldn't have anticipated that many years later, under a setting sun in a foreign country, I would finally understand the meaning of lost and found cat posters in my life and why Holly's story, in particular, swirled around inside of me. In the beginning I only wondered: What, besides love, had driven her to such lengths, all for Eccles, who would walk on the wild side into perpetuity?

A month later I spoke to Holly again; I needed a few points clarified. I'm glad I called. Things had changed.

"I think I know what happened," she said. A kick had returned to her voice. "Eccles wandered further than ever before into the Ridge Road area. It's on the other side of the park, but I didn't put any posters there. I'd never had to search there before." Eccles may have wandered so far, she hypothesized, that he was too lost to find his way back to the more familiar side of the park. I stifled an impulse to say something about denial and grieving.

In psychotherapy there's a term called *therapist neutrality.* Basically, it means don't interfere with a client's decision, unless he or she is headed for immediate destruction. That's the professional explanation for why I backed off and only offered a "Good luck!" But the real reason is more complicated, absurd, and messy. The concept of therapist neutrality isn't what leaped into my head when I heard about Holly's new plan. *Star Trek* did. I was a shrink who found guidance in reruns. The *Star Trek* doctrine, known within the show's universe as the "Prime Directive," dictates that one is not to interfere in the decision-making of other cultures or indigenous belief systems unless one's own planet is facing imminent devastation. It's a respectful philosophy, and empathic of other peoples' beliefs. I try to keep it in mind.

During any therapy session I have to make split-second decisions: Which fork in the road to take? Should I follow up on what the client just said? Steer the conversation to an earlier topic? Allow the silence to persist? Drift along in lightweight conversation? Let someone chew on the pros and cons of a decision? Should I allow a rigid client to stay confused because it's ultimately going to be more therapeutic than imposing a short-term sense of order? Should I make practical plans with a touchy-feely client who typically avoids thinking decisively and proactively?

Who was I to judge Holly's intuitions of the future? She was a capable, loving woman, full of passion and with a strong sense of community. She knew how to make decisions. What did I know? Prime Directive aside, I liked the freedom I was giving myself. I don't have to have the answers whether I'm a cat poster sleuth or a therapist or a regular person. It freed me to ask the question with genuine curiosity: What did I really know about Holly and Eccles?

After I organized the fragments of their story into a whole, the answer was surprisingly simple. They had an epic relationship. It defied absences, reunions, vanishings, accidents, depression, travel, serendipity, coincidence, the kindness of strangers, illness, longing, and an endless cycle of relationship building—surrender, acceptance, loss, and wandering. Holly wanders, searching for Eccles. Eccles wanders, pulled ahead by the duality of his nature. Holly's rebooted search could have been a brilliant idea, and it could have been an avoidance of the inevitable. I was following the Prime Directive. I cast no vote. I've practiced psychotherapy for twenty-five years and I can't explain what goes on, ultimately, between two people, let alone between animals and humans. The future wasn't mine to predict.

please call
(343)
555-
8239
DRIVEN
AWAY
BY
EVIL
Neighbor
CAT.
Pearl ST.
Area.
ANSWERS to "WUSS!

WUSS

Wuss, apparently, got his ass kicked. He wasn't just missing. He had been forced to flee his home and all that he loved. It was bad enough that he was bullied, but on top of that grand humiliation he wasn't allowed to even keep it a secret. His mother had essentially decided to broadcast the details of his smackdown and illustrated them, too, for our entire neighborhood. Friend and foe alike, people minding their own business, any visitor who parked a car on the street, the school kids, the happy hour customers, even the nuns at the Polish church, and the possum family in my yard were witness to his disgrace. He'd been "Driven away by evil neighbor cat." *Snicker.*

It was during my first year of sleuthing that I learned of Wuss's plight. I had stepped onto my porch with a morning cup of tea when I saw a lost-cat poster hanging on the pine near the sidewalk. I ambled down the sunny stairs—Nancy Drew eager to be helpful—and imagined returning him to an eternally grateful owner. As I drew closer, I read the words, "Driven away by evil neighbor cat."

Lost-cat posters were blooming in my neighborhood: *New to area. Doesn't know the neighborhood. Never been outdoors.* Fall, winter, and summer, faculty and students move in and out.

Double-parked Hondas and SUVs line the streets filled with boxes, clothes, and scrappy coffee tables. After a week of loud noises and furniture rearrangement the cats can't take it anymore. They split. And now, in addition to all that, Wuss had to put up with a bully cat. Oh, Wuss.

I took the poster off the tree and hustled back into the house to show my partner, Karis. "I found a poster!" I yelled to her. "It's epic." Karis and I had met about six months after Zak's rescue. She managed a restaurant, while she mulled over which graduate school to apply to. While she was deciding whether to major in English or psychology, I was already established in my second career—cat-poster sleuthing.

Karis was in the living room and she was strumming her guitar while rehearsing an old Frank Sinatra torch song.

"At your age, shouldn't you be singing a Bon Jovi song?" I teased. We were always amused by the generation gap in our Baby Boomer meets Slacker relationship.

"Poor Wuss," she said as she reached for the poster. "But wait, who names their cat 'Wuss'? Isn't that a guarantee that he's going to get beat up on the playground?"

Karis had arrived on the planet with wit, wisdom, and heart already intact. On her own since she was eighteen, she worked full time while putting herself through college. She loved cats. She'd named her own cat Shostakovich—Shasta for short—after the Russian composer. How did she come up with that name? "Inspiration," she said, mischievously. "Doesn't he look Russian?"

Poor Wuss. He could have used a tough-sounding Russian name.

Karis and I studied the illustration more thoroughly. Wuss was the black cat, but something orange and menacing stood behind him. What was it? Man or feline? It was upright and its mouth was open and its arms flailed dangerously close to the black cat. But the word "clothing" was printed next to the orange figure's head. What did that mean? What kind of cat wears clothes?

Perhaps the menacing creature was a person. Still if a person must chase a cat, clothing—in my neighborhood, even during July—is not optional. I wracked my brain for another explanation. Maybe clothing referred to an orange jumpsuit. If this was true, Wuss had been run out of town by an escaped convict.

The next day, Karis and I discovered a second poster hanging on a telephone pole around the corner. This one looked like a stripped-down version—only the picture of a black-and-white cat remained. However, new text had been added, which described the evil cat as orange. Zak was orange. Was he was in trouble again? This had been a rough year. Recovering from a catnapping, and now accused of feline felony assault. "Zak has no choice but to get out of town," Karis said. "He's an outdoor cat; he could never do hard time."

I was eager to call the owner.

Tara answered the phone, jumping into the conversation with the pride of a mother lion defending her cubs. "We had a ritual," she said. Tara explained that she was a graduate student at Yale and that every day she would walk to and from campus. "Wuss waited for me faithfully at the end of the driveway," she said with pride. "Then, out of the blue, this mean cat just showed up. He hissed and sneered constantly. He scared Wuss right out of his own yard. He's a bully, just awful. I hate him."

I held out hope that our cats would be able to avoid a turf war and everything that came with it. Wearing baggy jeans with my underwear showing was a fashion statement I wasn't prepared to make.

Then Tara testified to his state of mind. "Wuss was scared," she said. "He doesn't like confrontation. Some cats are just gentle." I could hear it in the sharpness of her voice. She was incredulous—survival of the fittest is no way to run a universe.

At the end of the driveway, Wuss had tried to take a stand

against the orange interloper, but his little squeaks were topped by the bully's growl. Initially, Wuss refused to cede his ground, but he was ceding emotionally. By day's end, Wuss's frontline had retreated to the front stoop. There was sustained troop movement overnight, and by morning, the orange menace had planted his flag. Wuss's itinerary for the day was rather limited: breakfast, followed by a cautious stride down the stairs, and a subsequent chase into exile.

I tried to get the lowdown on Wuss's lifestyle. From prior experiences I'd put together an informal list of questions to ask the owners. It's a basic journalism technique. Who? What? Where? When? Why? *Tell me about you and your cat. What happened right before the cat disappeared and during the search? Where did you search? When? Why do you think this happened?*

"Was Wuss mostly an indoor cat or an outdoor cat?" I asked. "Or was he a mix of the two?"

"Why should he have to stay inside?" Tara retorted, as if I'd challenged her cat's civil rights. "It's his yard." Then she laughed. "But it's not even that big of a yard. The orange cat should have taken over an estate, something worth fighting for.

"When I saw that he wasn't in the driveway," she continued, "I knew what had happened. It was that vicious cat. I put signs up that night, right away, and went searching. Of course, I bump into the orange cat." Almost inaudibly, she laughed. "That meant Wuss wasn't close-by. I took a flashlight and walked the streets of the neighborhood, but it felt so random. What were the chances that I'd flash a light on the bush where Wuss was hiding? Everybody has hedges around their house. I went home." Her lack of momentum seemed peculiar for someone so fiercely protective of her furry boy. Was her passion and pride defending against feelings of helplessness?

Many lost-cat owners describe an almost unstoppable energy, waning only after repeated failures. They typically search before and after work, and late at night. They speak with their neighbors, revisit the same places—under porches, cars, and bushes—and then get a sudden urge to search in a new area. Inside their home, owners will compulsively recheck rooms, tear apart cabinets and drawers, and examine kitchen pots and pans, closets, bedding, and hideaways.

"I hate the bully cat," Tara said, adding a self-reflective groan at the end. I, too, would hate any cat that chased my Zak away (but, I thought with devilish pride, Zak wouldn't have to run).

In the second black-and-white poster, besides describing the bully cat as orange, Tara had added some background details about Wuss. He was a "small, defenseless cat." Injustice gnawed at her.

However, the black cat she'd used in both posters was a Xerox from a Jonny Cat kitty litter bag. "It looked like Wuss," she purred. Mid-chuckle, I stopped laughing. Zak wasn't going to take the rap for beating up a graphic imposter.

Tara wasn't a novice lost-cat owner. She had used the Jonny Cat image before, which explained some of her resistance to roaming in the dark, as well as her "been there, done that" attitude. A few years earlier, Tara had another cat, also black and white, which had vanished. A lady living down the street had rescued her Jonny look-alike, but Tara never learned the whole story of her cat's disappearance. The rescuer didn't speak English.

"Why do you think one stray cat could chase another cat out of his own yard?" I asked casually.

"The orange cat hissed all the time," Tara said, her ferocity rising. "I'm telling you, Wuss *had* to run away from his own home."

At least Tara's description of the bully as a "hisser" relieved me of any personal responsibility. Zak didn't hiss, unless faced with an aggressive dog. He purred loudly, but none of the other neighborhood cats, that napped alongside him on my hot tub cover, seemed to be perturbed.

And then Tara got lucky.

"A couple of days later," she said, "magic or the Good Witch finally overpowered the bully and, thank God, he disappeared. Maybe he's bothering some other neighborhood now." But Wuss didn't hear the news. "He might have gotten lost," Tara said. "Two full days passed before I found him—waiting for me at the end of the driveway."

"Any scars?" I asked.

"No, he's still sweet," Tara said, dropping into a small, soft voice. I knew that voice. It's the voice we all use when we're alone and talking to our cat, when our adult persona has fallen so far back in time that we might need training wheels again. It's the voice of pure pleasure and lack of self-consciousness, when words don't have to be clever or precise or sophisticated. When naming a feeling is easy and doesn't require the help of a psychologist, an insurance company, and an hour a week to identify emotions because, honestly, we don't know what they are anymore. It's a voice we use when we caress our cats and kiss them on the nose, the one we use before we learn to hide our innocence with clever defenses. We need to safeguard that voice. And it's one of the hardest things in the world, figuring out how to keep that voice alive while developing a voice of reason, the one that's going to get us through the day and through our lives. The psychotherapist had kicked in.

I was puzzled, too. Where was the voice that would explain some of Tara's decisions? Why, before Wuss went missing, had she allowed her gentle cat to go outside when the bully, the day before, had literally forced him to cower by the front door?

I sensed a subtle conflict in the shadows. Pride often masquerades as other emotions, like anger and hurt. Pride can also be hidden inside of opinions and judgments. It can be difficult to detect, even in yourself. Forbidding Wuss to leave the house may have felt like a personal defeat for Tara—she couldn't stop "the injustice of it all," or even tolerate feeling powerless. It shouldn't be happening to her or Wuss!

And an unconscious truth also held sway: because she loved him, she believed that she could control the outcome and override certain realities. Love will keep our ritual intact. It will keep my cat safe. That's what people universally want their love to do—provide implicit control and protection. The manner in which we offer our protection is a matter of personality and style. In order to rescue Zak I followed chance into the unknown. Tara was counting on justice to prevail. Deep down, we were more alike than different. In the commotion of living, we want, through the power of our love, to keep our loved ones safe. Then we will never lose them.

Pride can be a difficult emotion to understand in ourselves, even when we are on the verge of losing someone we love. Pride hides in our distorted reasoning. We don't like to feel hurt or helpless in relationships. To escape our grief, we turn our conflicts into a mental exercise between right and wrong. We spend our time judging who has been right, who has been wrong. Blame feels empowering and offers temporary relief from feeling vulnerable. And we're all vulnerable.

High-spirited and intelligent, Tara reminded me of Jack, a handsome executive who'd contacted me for therapy during a personal crisis. At our first session, Jack pummeled the air with pseudo-insights about why his wife of fourteen years was planning to leave him. After half an hour, I suggested that Jack sit quietly and close his eyes. He was a polite person, so he agreed to do it, but then he pointed his chin outward. Twenty seconds later, I asked him, "What are you thinking or feeling?" Blinking his eyes open, he said, "How much this is costing me by the minute."

"Let's skip the math," I said. "Can you feel your contempt for me?" At first he denied it, but I assured him that I wasn't making a judgment. I explained, "You're hiding your real feelings behind pride. If you didn't cut me down or blame your wife, what might you feel?"

He sat quietly, his eyes bewildered. A few minutes later he dropped his chin and said, "I don't want to be alone."

"Is this an example of how you behave when you need someone?"

"I get sarcastic."

"How does Angela handle your dismissiveness?" I asked.

"She says she can never pin me down and then reminds me of what a great wife she's been."

"The two of you fight with pride," I said. "Do you ever fight about the real issues?"

"She tries," Jack said, and chuckled. "Once when I was mad I told Angela that our two collies love me more than they love her." He paused. "The thing is, I do love her."

The irony of my own pride did not escape me. Adding Wuss's multicolored poster raised the caliber of my collection. I was eager for the artistic details.

"And the poster, was that a man, or a cat, or the devil?" I asked Tara.

"An artist friend made it," Tara said. "I gave her the Jonny Cat image, but the rest was up to her. It's very creative, don't you think?"

"If you had an assistant helping you," I said, feeling surprised by the expert talent brought in for the task, "how come she wrote 'evil neighbor cat'?"

"Because he was," she said, amused.

"No other factors?" I was waiting for a deeper explanation, something with metaphor or artistic license. Maybe surrealism had stepped in. The orange had a red undertone, and red is the color of the devil. Some people consider the devil and evil to be the same thing. Perhaps Wuss was being chased by the concept, not the presence, of evil?

"Nope."

"How did Wuss get his name?"

"I like it."

"No other factors?"

Not every question finds a home, but Wuss had found his. He'd resumed his official title: Prince at the End of the Driveway.

I crowned Wuss's poster "The Best Cat Poster Ever" and stuck it on the bulletin board in the kitchen.

Karis walked in with a page of scribbled notes. "Are you struggling with grad school?" I asked.

"The timeshare we bought," she said, holding in a laugh, "is a bit restrictive. We won't be vacationing in the tropics. Only Montana in February is available."

"What will we do there?" I asked.

"Get some fresh air?"

Karis and I began our adventure by scanning clothing catalogs and going on shopping trips—snow boots, long underwear, ski pants, and the like. And as our departure date drew nearer, we looked forward to hiking and cross-country skiing. But how were two city girls like ourselves going to survive out in the woods? We didn't have a comprehensive skill set. Sure, I knew how to hail a cab in the rain, but I knew very little about the great outdoors— what about bears? I didn't want "Run faster" to be my last words. I planned on throwing my American Express card at the bear and yelling, "You can eat anytime, anywhere!"

LOST   CAT

Still missing as of January 30th

Maddy, Blue Sky Leather Shop cat
was lost the night of November 28th in the parking
lot of the mall.... She was seen shortly after
at the factory buildings. Have had reports of sightings
in December in the NE area of town.
She could be anywhere!
We are not ready to give up on her!
Any information please call (818) 555-3459.

THANK YOU!

MONTANA MADDY

I'm a dog person," said the woman seated next to me at the airport bar.

That wasn't the answer I was expecting.

Torrential rains had grounded all the planes in Minneapolis/St. Paul. I was stuck in the airport on a flight to Seattle, six months after finding a lost-cat poster while vacationing in Montana. With hours to kill, I decided to test some of my budding theories about lost-cat posters. After a year of sleuthing, I wondered if I had an entirely different relationship to lost-cat posters than Jane and John Q. Public or if they looked at them with the same scrutiny that I did.

When I read a lost-cat poster, I glean whatever information I can from its composition, then apply my intuition and experience to create a loose profile of the owner. Is the text simple and unadorned, or is it emotionally laden? Phrases such as "love her so much," "worried about his health," and "never been outdoors before" suggest the poster was written by a female. Women also pour on protective types of descriptions such as "afraid of loud noises" and "likes to hide." Pronouns are revealing: "I," "we," and "our" imply single or multiple owners. Hand drawings of kittens that resemble spotted cows delineate the child from the adult owner. Males, in general, tend to make declarative statements. ("Missing!" "Reward!" "Call!") They'll scan a photograph of the cat onto a poster, then add functional information such as street names, the time of disappearance, color of the cat, and age. The lengthy biography is usually missing. Fathers of young children are the exception to the rule. They may write emotional lines such as: "my daughter is sad," "my family misses her," and "the kids grew up with the cat."

Elizabeth had just identified herself as a "dog person," and as we drank wine and waited for the sun to come out, I made her my impromptu research subject. She was the director of a gallery for women artists in the West, a former New Yorker traveling to Arkansas to visit her fiancé. But Elizabeth came with complications. *What,* I wondered, *do non-cat people observe upon reading a lost-cat poster?*

"Because you are a dog person, does that mean if you saw a lost-cat poster you wouldn't read it?"

"Oh, no," she said. "I want people to be reunited with their pets."

I continued. "What do you think the owners might be like?" She looked at the poster then, and cautiously at me. I smiled again and tried to see myself as she saw me. I know that my brown eyes are considered piercing by some, passionate by others. Like most people, I have my own fears of not being liked, but I'm spontaneous and something of a fast talker, and that can make me appear more confident than I'm feeling on the inside. I tried to seem approachable, "I'm a cat owner and, once, I had to make a poster. Do you have a sense about the owners?"

About ten seconds later, she said, "They own a business. The poster mentions a shop."

"Any intuitions about the owner's gender or personality or temperament?" I wondered if a second glass of wine would make it easier for her to answer my unusual questions.

"Man." Elizabeth said slowly. "The poster is very factual. It's like a report."

"If the owner had written the words 'heartbroken' or 'desperate,' would that have drawn you in?" I asked, surprised by her conclusion.

"Oh, yes."

Was my barmate representative of the masses? Had Maddy's poster failed to convey personal anguish? A quick poll was in order. I asked the waitress to read the poster. She made a sad face and wanted to know if the cat had been found. Could she make any guesses about the owner's emotions? "Not really," she said. I moved on to the bartender. He probably knew how to read people. "The owners are logical types," he said. "Not the type to get emotional." I was surprised by their reactions.

According to the poster, the owners had been able to intermittently track the course of Maddy's disappearance, which took place on the night of November 12, in the parking lot of the mall. Not long after that she was seen near a local factory. In December, the search expanded to include the northeast section of town. But after hanging up a lost-cat poster and announcing to the world that they needed all the help they could get, because after *two months* of searching for Maddy they would, unfortunately, have to press on, and despite employing phrases such as "still missing" and "not ready to give up on her" and "could be anywhere" and "any information" and "please call," and even though they'd punctuated their call for help with a giant, capitalized "THANK YOU," somehow, the owners still hadn't adequately expressed their emotions, according to a "dog person."

Maddy was no slouch. She had a day job. It was long and official sounding: "The Blue Sky Leather Shop Cat." The poster showed her guarding the handle of a glass pitcher. Although the photograph was a bit blurry, Maddy still radiated an aura of dependability. She was a full-bodied gal, and obviously very pretty.

Her owner's name wasn't listed on the poster, but it was more than likely that the leather shop was run by a woman, since more of the stores and gift shops appeared to be. The words, "We are not ready to give up on her," heralded two months of determination and devotion.

Unfortunately, I hadn't been able to connect with the owner while Karis and I were vacationing in Montana. We spoke only after I'd returned to New Haven. It was then that I heard Alice's odyssey.

Let's start with the basics. Alice had left California decades ago for a rural life in Montana. Somehow it seemed as if she'd brought the innocence of the 1970s with her. She drove an old van with a bumper sticker slapped on it that read: UPPITTY WOMEN UNITE. I half expected her to be wearing an original tie-dye shirt. The "we" in the poster referred to her employees, who also adored the silver-and-white beauty. Alice adored Maddy. But when the eight-year-old cat disappeared, she blamed only herself. "I should have been more careful," she told me.

One afternoon, weeks after Maddy disappeared, a forlorn Alice was sitting at home watching the sun fade behind the mountains. The phone rang.

"I saw your Maddy kitty on the playground." It was a little girl, her words bopping out in a singsong rhythm. "She came up to me," the child continued.

"At most, she didn't sound more than nine or ten years old," Alice told me. "No kids had ever called before, but obviously she knew how to read. I tried to get details."

She asked the girl several times, "Where did you see Maddy?"

"I like kitties," the girl replied. "Yeah."

"Do you remember the day?" Alice asked. Then she offered the girl a more focused question. "Wednesday or Thursday?"

"I dunno," the girl said. "She came up to me."

Trying to find an entry point into a child's mind, Alice reduced the conversation to skeletal simplicity. "What's your name?" Some rambling remarks later, Alice left that behind and instead asked, "What color is the cat?"

"I pet her and she likes it," the girl said, making it an official conversation to nowhere.

"I didn't know what to think," Alice told me. "Was the girl deliberately vague? Or maybe she couldn't answer?" Alice paused. "Maybe she was telling the truth," she said, tripping on the last word.

The girl had eventually babbled something that sounded like the name of a local elementary school. Intent on discovering the girl's identity and not quite adept at distinguishing real gold from fool's gold, Alice made plans to visit the school the following afternoon. Perhaps face-to-face the girl would be less shy and more forthcoming. I wondered about this approach. Alice was going to just drop by the school? When was the last time she'd stepped foot in an elementary school? They have rules about these things.

The next day, Alice approached two teachers on the playground during recess. Did they know and would they please point out the little girl who'd found a stray cat? The teachers apprised her of the school policy: only a legal guardian may speak with a child. "I felt a bit rusty standing there," Judy said. "Though, the teachers were sympathetic, and they said that regardless of the rules, they had no idea who the girl was."

If the story had been true, the teachers added, the other students would certainly have crowded around a stray cat on the playground. Alice should have dropped the whole thing, particularly after she learned that the school also forbids interaction with any animal found wandering on the grounds, due to the possibility of disease. "It seemed like the girl made up the story," she said, sighing into the phone. "But why would a kid lie? Maybe she didn't. I couldn't tell what was true." I understood her indecision. A lost-cat owner wants to believe in magical thinking, too.

It had been Karis and our friend Alec who had spotted Maddy's poster on the door at the diner. They raced back to the timeshare condo to take me out for breakfast. "We saw this great cat poster!"

We pushed the door open and walked into the local diner. All two-legged creatures turned and stared at us. Yes, we were wearing black this and black that, but come on, I was also wearing a purple scarf with matching earmuffs, and Alec was looking sharp in a blue turtleneck. Karis always looked lovely. Across her forehead a mane of long chestnut hair fell to one side framing her large green eyes.

A few women were seated in the diner, but mostly it was filled with men wearing sweatshirts and baseball caps, their skin worn from the dry air. They crushed their cigarettes out in the dirty dishes and lit up again. We received endless refills of secondhand smoke. "You can't go to graduate school in Montana," I told Karis. "We can't afford the chemo."

To avoid the gaze of the diners, I buried my head in the local paper and found my favorite personal ad:

Motorcyclist, skier, looking for woman to leave this prison planet and join me in the back country for wilderness living.

But it was the lost-cat poster that really held my attention.

I called Alice shortly after leaving the diner. No one picked up. Experience had taught me that cat owners in distress aren't going to call a writer back, so when the answering machine clicked, I made a new plan—drop by the shop, buy a leather bag, and chat about Maddy.

But no one seemed to know where the shop was actually located. While Alice chased after Maddy, I chased after Alice. Each Montana native that I spoke with failed to recognize the name of the shop, but cheerfully made a guess as to its location. The search reached its nadir when I stopped my rental car to ask a silver-haired gentleman who was power walking down the street. He looked at me with brilliant blue eyes and announced, "Been living here fifty years, never heard of it."

"How hard can it be to find a leather shop in a small town?" Karis said. "And if it's that hard, maybe Maddy can't find it, either."

On the morning of my flight out, I asked the owner of a rifle shop for help. His cowboy hat tilted left across the street toward a peeling, orange-colored, one-room, crooked shack. It looked like the Big Bad Wolf from "The Three Little Pigs" story had blown down all the shop signs and was, for some reason, with-holding that last demolishing huff. We drove across the street. A lost-cat poster was taped on the glass, but the shop was closed. I stuck my nose against the window and peered in. It looked like a working studio. No frills, but plenty of shelving with large and small bags on display. Large pieces of raw leather lay under the workbench. In the backyard, old car parts and discarded chairs were rusting under the sun.

When Alice and I finally spoke. I pictured her in her shop, the phone tucked under her chin as she maneuvered her way around the crowded shelves. Her ordeal began on a routine drive to the supermarket. Alice didn't know she had a passenger until Maddy popped her head up from underneath the driver's seat. "I should have turned around right then and there, but I was in a hurry," she said. "I never dreamt she'd bolt."

Alice bought a few things and drove back to the shop, but Maddy didn't hop out of the van. *She'll come out at her own pace,* Alice thought, and left the van door open. The following morn-ing, she drove to the leather shop, but didn't find Maddy meow-ing at the back door to be let in. She had a sick feeling and sped to the supermarket to look for her. "Oh, my gosh," Alice said. "It's like somebody dumped their cat off in a strange parking lot, only it was me." She asked the manager for the names of the employees who'd worked the evening shift and returned that night to question them. They hadn't seen Maddy.

Alice made her first round of lost-cat posters and searched on the Internet for help. Nowadays an owner can type in "lost cat or missing cat" and find nonprofit organizations and businesses offering advice and services. They teach you how to design a poster, search effectively, and use humane Havahart traps. The trap is similar to a cage, but has three stable walls, with a movable fourth wall. The traps come in all sizes, depending on the animal that you need to capture. Pick your desired height for squirrels, weasels, and other "nuisance animals." And there's a perfect cat-sized trap, too. These mesh and wire traps come with detailed instructions and are specially designed to prevent injuries to animals—hence the name, Havahart ("have a heart").

Alice's plan was simple: lure Maddy with her favorite food, and once she stepped inside the small, metal trap, a wall would drop down keeping her safely inside. Well, that was the idea. "I was a failure," Alice said. "A complete and utter failure." She was an artist, not a mechanic. The diagrams gave her a headache. "I never caught anything, and adding insult to injury," she said with a laugh, "even the mice were eating the goods and then leaving."

Fortified with emotional support from a chat room, Alice expanded her radius by wading into the grassy fields behind the mall, arriving at several factories set back from the main road. The manager was friendly. Would he post Maddy's picture on the wall? "Sure," he said.

In the meantime, Alice was walking and talking her way through town, leaving a poster wherever she could. Two weeks later, she decided to revisit the factories. It was her dream come true! The employees had seen Maddy several times. For a split second, Alice heard what she'd been praying for. But there's more than one split in a second.

They said they hadn't known that her cat was *missing*. There wasn't now, nor had there ever been, a lost-cat poster hanging in the break room. "My heart sank," she told me. "The manager lied. Maddy could have been rescued. You have to be so aggressive. Nobody cares except you."

I didn't want to interrupt her, and I wasn't sure what to do with the information. All of us, at times, wonder who will help us in a crisis? It's our greatest hope that they will. And it's our greatest fear that they won't. The therapist-turned-sleuth was beginning to see that the search for a missing cat was also the story of how an owner was helped or hindered by her immediate world. In Alice's case, the manager's actions represented much more than simply the deeds of one man. They confirmed her prior worldview: "Nobody cares except you." Something in the past must have left a scar. Like all of us, when we're under great stress, Alice's dormant wounds had woken up with a roar.

In my role as cat sleuth, I was learning that when you talk to people about their animals, they'll often reveal personal and profound statements about their life. I was particularly glad that Alice and I were speaking and hoped that, in some small way, I was helping. Maybe some balance was being restored for her.

But Alice was running out of determination. Occasionally a well-wisher would call with a sighting; nevertheless, the search was at a standstill. The only saving grace was the unusually warm weather that year. It was after two months of dead ends when she received her first phone call from the little girl. Hope scurried down the rabbit hole, and Alice closed her eyes while free falling—Maddy was on the playground.

She tried not to dwell on the schoolyard fiasco. But three days later, the girl called her again. "I took the kitty on the bus home," she said. Alice was flummoxed. The kid was taking the lost-kitty act to a whole new level. Again, the conversation was an unsatisfying series of non sequiturs. Through conversation with townspeople, Alice learned that the school bus driver's wife had a friend who, coincidentally, had just bought a pocketbook at the shop. Her phone number was on the check.

Alice made a few calls. The bus driver's cameo was the last scene of the third act—"All the kids would be in a ruckus if a cat was on the bus."

"I guess the girl made things up," she said, without blame, "not realizing how much it might hurt the other person."

The girl's motivation was, indeed, curious. I tried to make sense of it.

One way of understanding why children lie is to see it as a means for youngsters to develop their own conscience. Lying is a necessary step in learning to be an individual instead of an extension of our parents. In this framework, lying would be a sign of autonomy. *Did you go to bed on time?* Yes! (I read under the blanket with my flashlight.) *Did you hit your brother?* No! (He deserved it.) *Did you do your homework?* Yes! (I plan on doing it, later, after this TV show.) Research suggests that one of the reasons that children lie is because they can get away with it, and success breeds more lying. They embellish and expand upon the original deceit.

But this little girl hadn't lied after being caught red-handed. She hadn't lied by omission, either. What had motivated her? She'd sought out the attention of an adult, yet hadn't responded to Alice's simple questions. The nature of her second phone call was similar to the first. She'd talked mainly about herself without revealing anything of substance. Why did she pretend to find Maddy? Did making the call help her feel important? Was she lonely? In general, when I try to understand children, I initially attribute the simplest motives to their behavior. I'm by no means a child therapist, but kids often do what they do for very concrete reasons—to get attention or to avoid it.

Even though Maddy seemed to be the reason the child was calling, she didn't have much to say about the cat. But where did she place herself in her fantasies? She was in the vicinity of other school children her age, who presumably were playing with one another on the playground and on the bus. Maybe no one's playing with this little girl, but she longs for companionship. Finally, in her imagination someone picks her, someone needs her. "Maddy came up to me."

Anxious kids have a difficult time in unstructured social situations involving other kids. They feel lost and invisible and prefer to be around adults. I think that when the little girl saw a lost-cat poster it was an unconscious fit for her. Lost kid, lost cat.

At the time of the incident, Alice hadn't even known the girl's name, but the bus driver's wife had eventually tracked it down. Someone, they feared, might take advantage of her vulnerabilities. They made a plan to speak with the girl's mother.

Alice's behavior was curious. She had no qualms whatsoever about chasing after people, looking up their numbers, calling them out of the blue, getting their numbers off checks, demanding the manager's names, trying to talk to a student on an elementary school playground, and beyond. She had moxie and resilience. At the same time, she had an air of inexperience, not unlike the little girl. I wanted to say to Alice, don't take your bad experience searching for Maddy as the ultimate lesson about all of life.

Sometimes people are simply disappointing.

Sometimes, life is.

While speaking with Alice, I had trouble deciding which of my two anecdotal cat-owner categories she belonged to. Cat owners, I'd come to realize, came in two sizes: regular and obsessive. These aren't fancy psychological terms.

Regulars show their love in the little ways, buying their cat's favorite foods or spreading catnip on the floor. A friend of mine lets her cat knead on her lap while she watches television. Regulars seem to understand that not everyone will share their love of kitty and his antics. After sharing one cute cat story, a regular will actually be aware of her audience's reaction. A regular will respond to drooping eyelids or a forced smile by ending story-telling time. Moreover, regulars don't expect their cat to be the owner's pal every moment of the day. They support their cat's need for alone time. Regulars have nicknames for their cats, of course, but they know the difference between public and private displays of affection. The vet knows your cat by his formal name, Buster. But at home, he's Little Boo Boo.

Obsessives are a different animal. They'll check all the same boxes as a regular (save for the part where they realize they're losing their audience), and they'll also gaze at their cat with the tenderness a mother bestows on her newborn. Obsessives will keep their cats indoors, monitoring their moods closely. Their homes are full of cat toys and cat beds, and when you visit them their conversation remains catcentric. "Look, Fluffy came into the doorway to check you out." One cute cat story may last as long as a Lifetime movie.

If you need to gauge your own position on the continuum ask yourself this: Do you feel happy playing with your cat? Does your self-esteem decline—only moderately—when your cat ig-nores your cooing calls. If so, you're likely a regular cat owner and a reasonable person. Most likely, you feel grateful when Fluffy sleeps on your bed, but you're also fairly certain that your cat has interviewed other potential owners.

If, on the other hand, you believe you know precisely what your cat is thinking. If you cry when your cat forgets your birthday, and if you've been known to ask your cat for fashion advice—"Do I look good in these jeans?"—then you, my friend, are an obsessive cat owner.

But details aside, the two categories are usually distinguished with a simple comparison: Obsessives will take a bullet for their cat; regulars will not. Alice was an easygoing regular type, but a crisis will turn any cat lover into an obsessive. I'd taken an entire round of ammo for Zak.

After three months Alice finally placed the call she never wanted to make—to the animal shelter. They had a few cats available for adoption. What kind of cat was she looking for? "A boy, short-haired and friendly." For some reason, the technician persisted—what was Alice's dream cat? "It's a tabby-point Siamese," she said. (The tabby-pointed cats, in contrast to the well-known dark markings of the traditional Siamese, have striped faces, legs, and tails). The technician put her on hold, and when he came back to the phone, he told her, "You're not going to believe this, but we have a young, neutered, tabby-pointed Siamese. Benny, who's being re-homed."

I was stumped by the word "re-homed." It loosely refers to returned merchandise, but at a shelter, it's an adoptive cat that gets returned: "Lease a preowned feline, guaranteed thirty-day affection plan!" Several weeks earlier, a farm couple had come to the shelter. They weren't looking for love. They wanted a barn cat that could catch mice. Maybe the farmers didn't grasp the nature of Siamese cats, or understand that the breed's lineage went all the way back to seventeenth-century royal Thailand. Either way, their adoptee had zero interest in chasing tiny critters for his keep, let alone calling the barn "home sweet home." He kept walking off the job and slipping in through the dog door. (Siamese don't like to be alone.) He got his pink slip and a free ride back to the shelter.

Many owners I spoke with in the midst of their search had also adopted homeless cats. One man spread kitty litter on his sidewalk so that his chocolate Siamese, Bosco, could smell his way home. He eventually did. After the reunion, he went back to the pound and adopted a second Siamese he'd met and fallen in love with while searching for his own. Alice felt that by getting a male cat, she was leaving room for both cats to get along. She took Benny home to the leather shop and saved a spot in the window for Maddy.

Over the course of our conversation, Alice turned inquisitive.

"What motivates you to call lost-cat owners? Did you lose a cat?" I gave a short, polite answer, the one I'd been reciting for cat owners the last year.

"I'd like to hear your story if you want to tell it," Alice said. I went with my instinct and shared how I'd come to enlist the services of a psychic. At the end of my story, in her friendly, oh-by-the-way voice, Alice said, "Yeah, I got in touch with three animal communicators."

The times were changing—now even psychics were reinventing their image.

Alice's next three searches included Heaven, Texas, and Ya-hoo! She sent a brief e-mail to the first animal communicator, asking if it was possible to barter leather goods for a reading. Leaving out the word "in," the woman wrote back, "I'm sorry to say your kitty is heaven." Alice repeated the peculiar phrase "is heaven."

"She hurt me," Alice said, "Someone would send a death announcement by e-mail? I wanted to know about bartering. That's all." I thought about calling up the psychic and reading her the rules of customer service. First: *Do no harm*. Second: *Get some empathy*. I'd wanted to discover how others had responded to the needs of lost-cat owners. Alice deserved better.

A friend convinced her to contact a second communicator, a woman living in Texas. The psychic wasn't sure if Maddy was dead or alive. Apparently, when a cat is displaced, it's difficult to get a clear reading because, energetically, the cat actually leaves its own body behind. The second psychic sensed something about a cat with a white-tip tail, but that described Benny, the Siamese. At the end of the reading, the communicator told her, "The cat you have is the one you're supposed to have."

"What a stock, New-Age answer," Alice said. "Anyone could have said that."

The third communicator seemed to have more psychic juice than the others. She told Alice that Maddy was definitely alive.

Using a Yahoo! map, she identified where Maddy had disappeared, but Alice had already figured that out, and there was nothing more the communicator could offer. The final tally: dead, maybe dead, or alive.

Sightings, stories, and psychics brought her close, but never close enough to grab Maddy and take her home. Alice returned to relying on herself. It seemed that despite all the players who'd become involved and the actions taken, she essentially felt unprotected. She felt at fault for her own loss. Despite her strength and best intentions, she felt helpless. I felt solidarity with Alice. It was March, and she continued to distribute flyers and search whenever someone called with new information. "I'm gonna have to let go," she confessed. "She's dead or she found a new home, or the person who kept her hasn't seen my ad. I know that I got Benny out of all of this, and I love him, but I love Maddy, too. I didn't want this to end up being some kind of twisted trade."

Originally, Benny's arrival in the shop had been a godsend for Alice, but now she needed a double shot of forgiveness: first for losing Maddy, and then for loving Benny. A twisted logic had taken over. The quantum physics of Maddy's reappearance had apparently been blocked by the presence of one striped Siamese, who currently occupied too much space in Alice's grieving heart.

Trying to trace the illogical connections that live inside of an otherwise high-functioning adult is the core job of a therapist. Therapy can help people to identify their feelings, but the real detective work is deciphering the irrational thoughts that have become associated with their feelings. During times of grief, irrational thinking multiplies. ("I didn't see my dad one last time." "I should have called.") In effect, we tell ourselves fanciful stories that we could change the pain of death and separation and longing if only we'd had the foresight to move one speck in the universe.

It's been my experience that people deserving of forgiveness are usually the last to grant it to themselves. Alice held a false belief: She'd not protected her cat well enough. Time had yet to turn into a remedy, washing away her guilty feelings, or a message of finality, releasing her from her odyssey for Maddy.

Despite her desire to be at peace, her struggle to let go wasn't over. Before we said good-bye, she muttered something about a sighting in a town more than a few miles away. Then she took a breath and said, "I'm going to check it out."

LOST - A VERY SHY BLACK
(PAWS + CHEST)
AND WHITE CAT NAMED
NIKA. IF SEEN, PLEASE
CALL (882) 555 - 6157. RAN AWAY FROM
ORANGE ST. FRIDAY PM

NIKO

Q: What do real estate and successful lost-cat posters have in common?
A: Location! Location! Location!

"Virgin," I said to Karis. We were staring at Niko's poster on the telephone pole. "I'm almost positive." After a year and a half of hard-core sleuthing, I'd seen enough missing-cat posters to conclude that Niko's owner wasn't exactly savvy. The poster lacked any and all conventional selling points; the public couldn't see that they'd been invited to care.

I only saw the poster because I'd bent down on the sidewalk to tie my bootlace. Several outdated flyers for rock bands had buried it from full view. The poster's placement broke the first rule of marketing: Make it easy for the customer to find you. Even without the competing posters, Niko's poster was doomed to obscurity. It wasn't facing in the direction of the oncoming traffic. A driver could only have seen it if he had a sudden urge to look back over his right shoulder. These were the goofs, I thought, of a frantic cat owner. I sympathized.

The location was handicapping the search for Niko, but there was even more. Most lost-cat owners make their posters using standard eight-and-a-half-by-eleven-inch sheets of white paper. The heading would be written in big, capital letters across the entire width of the poster. The public is familiar with this approach and readily recognizes the message. Niko's owner had entirely dispensed with tradition, and had fashioned a poster out of an odd-sized manila cardboard, skipped the bold heading, and tacked it awkwardly on its side. Rather than resting right side up, it seemed tipped over—the *Titanic* came to mind. I worried about the captain.

Judging by the date listed, the poster had been left to the elements for three months. Niko might still have been missing, or maybe the owner just hadn't bothered to take the poster down. I wasn't sure yet how timely owners were, in general, about updating or removing their posters.

"This is strange," Karis said. "Niko 'ran away.' Where's the public relations spin?"

No self-respecting cat owner would announce that their cat dissed them for the open road. You say, "lost," "scared," or "disappeared." You don't tell the world your cat dumped you, just so he could troll around.

"I was lucky," I told her, "When Zak was under house arrest, I knew at least that he still cared about me."

"What do you think of this crossed-out letter?" I asked Karis, pointing to the "k" in Niko that had been scribbled on top of what looked like the letter "m." "Who doesn't know how to spell their cat's name?" We stared at the poster.

"It's only got four letters," Karis said. "How can you mess that up?"

Given what we perceived to be the owner's level of anxiety, the fact that he or she had even managed to create a poster seemed a miracle. The poster practically blushed "this is my first time." Who made the sign? The handwriting was uneven. Perhaps it was a child. If so, we felt bad.

We continued walking in the bitter chill and tried to imagine who Niko was. He or she might have been an older cat, recently adopted—maybe "Nimo" was his legal name in his former life. Niko sounded foreign. Maybe the owner was Greek. How well did the sign maker know the cat? Then our wool-capped heads simultaneously snapped to attention, and we locked eyes.

The maker of the poster wasn't the owner!

This explained the advertising snafu, "ran away." We doubted the sign maker was even a cat person, because a real cat person certainly doesn't publicize that her cat is minimally attached to her. But at least the words "ran away" invites the public to the rescue. (I once saw a poster in Brooklyn for a cat named "Honey." In big red letters it said, STOLEN. Several days later the poster was replaced with a new one that said, MISSING! Although "stolen" may have represented the truth, no one is going to help if the reward may lead to a plea bargain or the phrase, "get your affairs in order.")

The next morning, before I'd had the chance to call the number listed on the poster, a cat-loving client of mine arrived for her appointment. I especially enjoyed my sessions with Deb. She was plotting to get off the middle-class grid. A handy mechanic, she'd purchased an RV, quit her job, and was hell-bent on hitting the open road. Working with Deb, I was learning about the subculture of rootlessness. It takes planning. (For instance, how do you apply for a license when you have no permanent address? *Answer:* North Dakota will issue a driver's license to a post-office box.) I learned about trailer design and repair. "Repair" being the operative word. Deb was a skilled mechanic. She introduced me to Web sites for the modern-day wanderer, portable plumbing gadgets, and which campgrounds barter parking fees for work exchange. All four of Deb's cats were going off the grid with her. She'd even researched the best type of tent for them and purchased floor-length screens with some solid walls, for those private moments.

When I opened the door to greet Deb, she put her forefinger

over her lips and then pointed over the porch railing. I could see in the bushes a black-and-white cat that looked very much like Niko. I hurried back to my office and grabbed the poster to make a comparison. The bush cat had the right markings, but this cat looked shiny and clean, not like it had been hiding all through the winter and scavenging for food. Sensing a possible kidnapping in the air, Niko, or his facsimile, quickly skittered down the driveway. We hustled after him and watched as he ran into the neighbor's evergreen trees as fast as Cary Grant ran from the crop duster in *North by Northwest*.

We walked back to my office and decided to call the number on the poster. "Hi, I have a black-and-white cat in the yard," I said. "He looks lost."

The friendly voice of an older woman cut in. "Ah, no, he's been found," she said, gratefully. "He wasn't even my cat!"

Bull's-eye!

"I was taking care of him for a neighbor," she said. "Can you imagine? I was just cat sitting, helping out. Then he took off."

"Did he sneak out?" I asked.

"He shot out like a bullet," she said. "It wasn't my fault. Niko's owner was in a pinch. He didn't have anyone to take care of the cat and asked if I could look after him." The owner had left on Christmas Day, and it was unclear how well he'd prepared for the trip. But I suspect that December was a month he knew about all year long, and his neighbor Helen had become the "I'm-not-paying-to-board-him" plan.

"I'm not even a cat person," Helen said anxiously. I took it to mean she didn't know anything about the care of cats. Then she added, almost confessionally, "I was just trying to be helpful. His owner said that the cat likes to sit in the apartment hallway. Well, wouldn't you know it? Somebody comes in the front door, and the cat bolts, right in front of me. I felt awful."

Helen quickly put together a rescue operation. "I sent out a search party and had some kids in the neighborhood look," she

said. "I put food on the back porch, and signs up on the streets."
Her back-up plan to save Niko was more worrisome. "It being
winter and all, I was hoping he could hook up with the other
roving cats in the neighborhood. They could hang out together.
If they'd accept him into the group, then he'd be okay."

Plan B sounded like a cat version of *Lord of the Flies*. If they
allowed this shy cat into the clan, he'd be okay. If they didn't,
they'd break his glasses and push him off a cliff.

But Niko's fate improved; he didn't have to go into group
therapy after all. He showed up at the front door two days later.
He must have weighed the odds—the warmth of captivity versus
wandering blindly at the bottom of the rocks. "He looked perky,"
Helen said. "I was lucky," she added, without sounding relieved.
"Lucky, otherwise I'm afraid to think of what would have happened. I'd have lost the neighbor's cat, and it would have been
my fault, too."

You didn't have to be a shrink to get the picture. Niko had
been rescued months ago, but Helen was still spinning on a
wheel of anxiety.

Anxiety and stress are the top two reasons people go into
therapy. It's a great catchall without stigma attached to it, and
it's accurate. Anxiety and stress are part of any issue—career,
love, marriage problems, caring for elderly parents—that will
motivate someone into therapy. However gender differences apply. Most men will self-describe as "stressed," while women ad-
mit to feeling anxious and depressed. Either way, underneath
the labels, the same lousy feelings and judgments exist—self-
blame, helplessness, shame, and so on.

How do you treat anxiety? Techniques such as following your
breathing and changing catastrophic thoughts into positive ones
can help. The chronically anxious, unfortunately, experience
their negative thoughts in rapid-fire succession and that can be
difficult to challenge. In therapy, it's my job to help my clients
change their framework. I use a sports metaphor. If you're a pole

vaulter, imagine yourself successfully leaping over the bar. You don't rehearse hitting the bar. I also have clients apply positive visualizations to their problem area (socializing, fear of leaving the house, etc.). Even a person in the midst of a full-blown panic attack—heart racing, sweating, dry mouth—can change his or her state of mind.

Although I'm a big proponent of exercise, healthy eating, meditation, and supplements, at times, they're just not enough. That's where medication can come in—as a tool to retrain the body. Medication slows down the body's excitable responses allowing the anxious person to stay calm enough to implement new thoughts. Side effects are important to consider, of course, and the decision to take medication shouldn't be made lightly. Still, the anti-medication contingent can be knuckleheaded. I'm used to clients saying, "I don't take medication, not even an aspirin."

"Really," I say. "Well, let's review. You're a high-functioning executive who smokes pot, drinks alcohol, and occasionally does a few lines. Once in a blue moon, you drop Ecstasy, too. So you don't take medication, unless it comes from the street and you have no idea what's in it."

Clients laugh at their own contradictions, and then the real issue comes into play: fear of the loss of control. They're afraid that medication will change what they *do* like about themselves. I reassure them. You will still like your favorite TV show. A Republican will *not* become a Democrat or, heaven forbid, a "dog person" will *not* turn into a "cat person." They resent, and I deeply understand this resentment, a pill having the power to repair what they want to be able to fix on their own. They feel shame.

I frame the issue of medications with biology. For example, it's like taking insulin for diabetes. It helps the pancreas. Some antidepressants and holistic formulas may reforest the parts of the brain that need re-seeding. And sometimes, after the brain regenerates what was missing, a client can stop taking the anti-depressant, unlike insulin, which must be taken daily, forever. Sometimes there is a placebo effect and people's symptoms may diminish not because of the drug per se, but because of the hope that goes along with taking it. In the short term, it offers a reprieve from distress while you learn new coping skills. Often, after resetting their own physical responses, learning to think more clearly, and successfully weathering stressful feelings, people can ease themselves off the medication.

I wanted Helen to feel better. But what would help her in the next two minutes? It was time for the Car Wash School of Therapy—the quick, economical package. Drive up anxious, get some insight, drive away feeling shiny and new.

Pre-soak her in reality.

"Helen, it's not your fault he ran away," I said.

"You don't think so?" she says.

I offered her a lighter perspective, "Niko started it."

"But the neighbor asked me," she said, missing the humor.

"It's the neighbor's responsibility to plan better," I said. "You did your best."

Driver blinded by suds. "I don't want anyone to be upset," she said nervously.

Helen was what's known as a *conflict avoider*. Because the overarching goal becomes not having anyone mad or disappointed, conflict avoiders are incapable of advocating for themselves.

"Well, give yourself credit," I said, realizing that Helen needed praise, not insight. "It was nice of you to help out."

Rinse cycle floods in. "You think so?" she said, calmly.

"Yes, definitely. You were very kind to fill in on such short notice."

Green light flashes. "Thank you. Thank you for calling me."

"You're so welcome."

"He isn't even my cat."

There it was, the wheel of anxiety spinning around as if she had no memory of the preceding exchange. Even a normally un-anxious person's brain will release adrenaline when shocked by an alarming event. Other chemicals and hormones will be generated, creating a heightened memory of the triggering experience. I understood the chemistry of Helen's anxiety, but I still wished that I could change it.

I empathize with people who lose their cool after years of trying to soothe their chronically anxious loved ones. Impatience, curtness, and sarcasm become our unedited responses. Of course, most of us don't intend to turn mean-spirited, but over the years, our feelings of defeat are acted out on the defeater. In time, we find ourselves in a place where we're not only aggravated by our loved one's seeming unwillingness to use logic or common sense, but our irritable reactions encourage their anxiety.

Few people are aware of how anxiety can masquerade as a normal part of someone's personality and character. "Oh, he's always complaining." "My wife's a scatterbrain." "He never has anything good to say." "She's just afraid to go on job interviews." "He can't sit still, that's his nature." "Ever since I was a kid, I've had trouble falling asleep." "She refuses to concentrate." "He drinks to calm down."

Partners often say, "I worry, because you don't care about the bills, the kids, etc," "I'm a chocoholic, carbohydrates love me," "She's a shopaholic," "He doesn't make friends too easily," or "He stays at work until the job's done." Even pleasure can be affected by chronic anxiety. ("I don't like vacations. I get bored.")

Some chronically anxious people may become defensive and/or passive-aggressive. They canonize their quirky adaptations. ("I like to be home before dark. Would you prefer I get into a car accident?")

Anxiety was in full force at a wedding reception I attended.

At the dinner table my name tag had been placed next to a man who compulsively tapped his foot against my chair. After he learned what I did for a living, he said, "Oh, so you think I'm a mental case?" In those moments, I wished that my job was teaching kindergarten. People would then hopefully smile sweetly instead of narrowing their pupils.

"No," I replied, hoping the band would get back from their break and drown out the conversation. "Dark Side of the Moon" seemed appropriate. "I'm listening to the story *you* brought up about your ex-wife." His nerves weren't going to pop the bubbles in my champagne. If only I could have sat next to someone more honest like Helen. Sure, she'd have been anxiously repeating herself, but at least she was fun to talk to. Her warm nature, however, contributed to her woes. Helpless to handle the anxiety associated with saying no, she was easily maneuvered into meeting other peoples' expectations.

"I've never seen a cat move so fast," she said, recalling a line from her list of indelible memories. "Just my luck, he shot out like a bullet."

I sighed warmly. I tried one last tactic. "If you were in prison for a crime, when would your sentence be over? Can you say that three months of guilt has paid for your crime of almost, *but not*, losing Niko?" She remained silent. That was progress. A moment of self-reflection, instead of automatic self-blame.

"Honestly," she said, as if we were in a confessional booth, "I don't want to babysit for a cat ever again. I'm not a cat person."

A week later, I met a professional cat sitter while sitting in my doctor's waiting room. After exchanging our own cat stories, I shared a few tidbits about Helen's school-of-wishful-thinking approach to rescue. "You can't expect to find anything by passively hanging up a poster," Kat said (an abbreviation for Katherine). "You have to talk to your neighbors, not just hope they'll take that extra step."

I agreed with her analysis. Then she took me to graduate school.

She surprised me by rummaging around the bottom of a large suitcase . . . or, umm, pocketbook and bringing out a wrinkled piece of paper folded in half. It was an old lost-cat poster for her orange cat Morris. "You know how I found him?"

"No clue."

"A lady in my neighborhood. I bumped into her on the street. I spent fifteen minutes with her, talking about her life, my life, and Morris. He's double pawed, see?" She pointed to his paws. "Because if she doesn't care about you, she's not gonna care about your cat. Understand?

"My boyfriend told me I was a pest," she said, tucking away the poster of Morris. "I bother people." She rolled her dark, Italian eyes at the idea of him. "He loves me and tells me I'm a pest. So what? That's a crime? I'm searching for someone I love. Why are people afraid to be considered pests? Be polite and never find your cat? That's a worse crime!"

I wanted to tell her that my mother would have been mighty proud of her. They were alike, both straight shooters. My mother always told her four kids, "You can find out anything. Just ask questions." She didn't grow up with Google, either. Curiosity was in her blood. When she needed to supplement my father's teaching salary she sold encyclopedias, *World Book,* door-to-door. Each volume corresponded to one letter in the alphabet. At twelve years old, I remember my twin brother, Richie, read volume G.

The lost-cat–poster sleuthing was a year and half old at this point. I'd learned dozens of ways to lose your cat—ripped screens, drunken roommates, gas leaks, open windows, moving-day horrors, and cats trying to find their old homes. Owners had great stories to tell. Lost-cat owners were friendly, even welcoming, and my curiosity was being deeply nourished. I'd heard complicated stories with endless twists and turns, but despite the tragedy of having to search for your missing cat, most owners, like me, had silly episodes and laughed at themselves. Ingenuity helped. And there's no escaping the crazy fears that run through your head.

I became fascinated by how different people coped with a similar calamity. Seemingly, each owner's temperament, history, personality, and spirituality influenced their responses to adversity. Without quite naming it at the time, I began to think about resilience. The owners needed it, and the cats, too. I thought back to Holly and Eccles. What made them so resilient?

I continued collecting posters in my half-aware state that I'd added some new questions. My protocol remained the same. After discovering the cat poster, and letting some time pass, I would cold-call the owner and speak to a complete stranger.

One evening, after a long day of work, I let my home phone ring without answering it. Several hours later I finally played back the message and immediately felt guilty. My brother's voice was restrained but distressed, "What's the best way to make a lost-cat poster?"

LOST CAT

Name: Tori
Type: Tortoise Shell
Age: 11 months, 3 weeks
Colors: Brown, Orange, White, Black
Last Seen: Early Saturday Morning, at 5:30 a.m.

IF FOUND, PLEASE CALL (233) 555-0121

TORI

"I don't want to talk to Valerie about death." My brother's voice was a throaty whisper. "But she's very upset," he said. "This is the first time the cat's gone out and not come back."

My seven-year-old niece had adopted her first kitten ten months earlier. The tag on the cage in the animal shelter said her name was "Torti"—a shortcut, it seemed, for the kitten's tortoise-shell coloring. But Valerie was having none of it. "That's a dumb name for a girl kitten," Val told me. She promptly changed it to "Tori."

Now Tori had disappeared, and Jeff wanted my help in designing a poster. At this point, my collection had inspired a number of devotees. Friends and family had taken to assessing and reviewing lost-cat posters on their own time, and they felt compelled to leave messages and critiques on my voicemail. ("Hey, there's a good one on Main Street. This cat is so handsome!" "You won't believe the poster I saw. . . .")

Old pals from across the country were finding posters, and a few enthusiasts were even mailing them to me. I was charmed whenever I received a poster from Beverly Hills or Seattle. But I'd created an informal code for my quest. Nancy Drew had to see the posters in their natural habitats. This way I could play my game more effectively: "Who is the owner?" I needed context. I'd learned that I had to observe the circumstances and setting of the poster (e.g., store window, city lamp post, a tree on a country road) and merge my intuitions with any identifying data.

But my priorities had shifted. This was personal. I had to help my brother—long distance—make a poster and find a missing furry relative. I switched into crisis-solving mode like an ER doctor doing triage. Jeff had never cared for a pet, and he knew next to nothing about cats. Meanwhile, an adolescent kitten was pawing her way through the busy streets of Chapel Hill. "Get a picture of Tori," I told Jeff, "and include Valerie in the poster-making process."

"Yeah," Jeff muttered. He seemed preoccupied.

"What else is bothering you? It's too soon to be discouraged. It's only been a day. Cats like to wander. That's their nature."

"Remember the Bunny thing?"

How could I forget?

When Valerie was six years old, she'd left Bunny, her stuffed rabbit from infancy, on the sink in one of the ladies's room at LaGuardia Airport. I'd met Bunny years earlier. He was skinny, with long arms, legs, and droopy ears. His scraggy, gray fur may have once been white. The most important information that I knew about Bunny was that he spoke only to Val.

At the airport they caught a taxi and drove into rush-hour traffic. A half hour into the ride, Val shouted, "I can't find Bunny." Jeff looked around the cab. "No," Val said, with horror, "I left him in the ladies room." Jeff wanted to sooth his daughter by reversing direction and wading through the Friday evening chaos at the airport, but doing so would create a different chaos by not meeting up with me (pre-cell phone era). Jeff reassured Val, that if Bunny was returned to the Lost and Found Department, they would rescue him before their flight on Sunday. Val cried for the entirety of the cab ride.

As we reminisced on the phone I realized that other than

sharing our feelings of having been in crisis, Jeff and I had entirely different recollections of the events that occurred during our lost-bunny weekend. He swears we had a rabbit-solving conversation at the Empire State Building. I remember only the fierce wind and buying Val a sweatshirt. Of course, Jeff remembers his sense of urgency as the dad and problem solver, the quandary he'd felt about not returning to the airport, all the phone calls that he placed to the airport, and the idea of buying an identical bunny. I worried about getting a replacement bunny; it wouldn't smell the same or be worn-down sloppy soft. I tried to be positive.

While Jeff and I waited to find out if the toy store had another rabbit in stock, we took Val on the ferry to see the Statue of Liberty. Later, when the news finally came that yes there was a replacement bunny, he and I nodded, a tiny flash of success. We had outmaneuvered this crisis, losing what you love.

"Good news," Jeff said as he hung up the phone, "we found an identical bunny!" Val smiled but she didn't say anything. A few minutes later, I saw a tear roll down her cheek.

"Sweetie, what's wrong?"

She looked down at the floor. "Thank you," she finally choked out, "but it's not the same bunny."

On Sunday, at Newark Airport, Valerie told the woman at the Lost and Found all about Bunny. When she went to look for him in another room, Val couldn't stop herself from partially following her. Shoved between a backpack and a shopping bag, legs kicked out in front of him, Bunny had waited for his family to post bail. "That's him!" Val yelled. "Bunny!"

Jeff said he'd never been so happy to see an inanimate object in his life. After they boarded the plane he took a picture of Val smiling in her seat, holding Bunny, and sent it to me.

"Remember the Bunny thing" was a reminder, and a battle cry: *Tori was missing!* It also conjured up feelings of helplessness. Jeff and I were in implicit agreement. Val was an only child and although she was close to both of her parents they were divorced. We didn't want her to lose anything else.

If we could have been entirely honest with ourselves at the time it was more complicated than losing a beloved stuffed animal. Long before the missing floppy-eared bunny or the missing long-haired calico, loss had already shaped my life, as well as the lives of my brothers. I didn't want to talk to Valerie about death, either. This loss was summoning up memories of other losses, and I started to miss my family.

When I was younger, my friends used to tell me that my parents were "interesting." They called my handsome, athletic father Tarzan. He was a vice principal of a middle school, and when emotionally troubled children ended up in his office, he would teach them how to juggle. He was a lifeguard in the summer, and he'd stand at the deep end of the pool, smiling Buddha-like, and challenge any combination of five kids and adults to dislodge him. My brothers tried their whole lives to knock him over. He played that same game all his life. He never lost.

Our athletic father died suddenly in his sleep. A year later, our older sister, Judy, died from a blood clot. She was thirty-one. Our grandparents, my favorite cousin, my brother's best friend . . . they'd all passed away.

My mother was complicated and unpredictable. She faced death like a warrior, flying from Connecticut to Los Angeles to close my sister's estate. Afterward, she called to say that she felt like taking a long drive in my sister's yellow Mustang. She needed to wander. This was before the availability of cell phones or GPS, and she was disappearing out West. I tried to discourage her, but I knew she'd made up her mind. She liked to drive and I knew she'd be safe. She was a loner. Where do you go when there is no solace to find? She'd gone missing.

I worried about her soul-splitting pain. I waited for her to come home.

Ten days later, she knocked on my front door in New Haven. "Where have you been?" I asked.

"I had to drive through the desert," she said, looking up at the sky, "and roll down the windows and scream at God: '*Why?*'"

Missing family members, friends, pets, and stuffed bunnies must rain from the same cloud of loss and unknowing. I may not have wanted Val to learn about death just yet, but I also didn't want to be one of those overprotective adults, the "helicopter" types who swoop in to ward off every potential hurt. And yet I still remembered when I was ten and my cat, Tiger, was run over in the street.

Tori, just come home.

Jeff ended up making the poster himself. It had a sweet picture of a poised, long-haired calico. I had to chuckle at the precision with which he described the cat's age—eleven months and three weeks. While Valerie slept, he drove up and down the neighborhood, taping Tori's picture onto telephone poles and trees. The next day, as Tori crept underneath the backyard evergreens, her own GPS system was guiding her back home. Her long hair tangled and twisted with twigs and leaves, she climbed the stairs and waited on the porch. When Jeff opened the back door to call her name, he found her at his feet. She scooted through his legs, past his six-foot-three-inch frame, and straight to the food bowl. Valerie woke up to find Tori curled up on the rug, sleeping off her adventure. She yelled out, "Daddy, Daddy, Tori's home!"

When I heard the good news, I was looking out the backyard kitchen window of the house I had bought eight years prior. White birch and towering pine trees loomed over ivy-covered garden walls, honeysuckle bushes, and late-blooming flowers. I often felt like I was sitting in a tiny English park. It was my own secret garden, hidden from the street, and it held memories of my mother.

I had dubbed my tiny eighteenth-century home "Skinny Acres." I bought the saddest-looking property on the street, twenty-three feet wide and one hundred feet deep. My mother, alone out of all my friends, agreed with my vision of the future. "You can make this place charming," she said, surveying the peeling paint and missing shingles.

She had vision, too, but she was born into the wrong era. Forced to drop out of college in the 1940s to help support her parents, she became a 1950s housewife, reading *The Wall Street Journal* at home, gambling, working part-time jobs, and serving us Chinese takeout for dinner. Instead of having kids, she should have gone into business or traveled the world or set up shop as a private detective.

What I remember most about my house is what never happened there, the life that I imagined I would provide for my mother after she moved in with me. I asked her to come live in my new house after she confessed that she was losing to her second round of breast cancer. I began remodeling the first floor of Skinny Acres to make it physically accessible for her in the months that we anticipated sharing together.

But that time never came to be. We lost our imagined future. Early one morning, a few weeks before her expected arrival, we'd been decorating her bedroom by phone. Later that evening I received a call from a nurse. My mother had difficulty breathing and admitted herself into the hospital. When I arrived at her bedside, she said, "I'm sorry. I can't come live with you."

It was a profound acknowledgment of how close we'd become. The need for love hadn't always propelled the best parts of me, but after Judy's death, the wary distance between us finally healed. My mother and I had not always understood each other. It wasn't for lack of love, but there are forces in life that tear you from the people you wish you could be close to.

Fourteen years old can be a tough time for most teenagers. You feel like an outsider and are anxious to understand who you are. I was particularly scared, but I felt compelled to learn about who I was and unable to resist its consequences. I went on a secret mission. I found the only book in my small-town library on homosexuality. It was written by doctors. "Lesbians are deviant, narcissistic, and incapable of loving." I sat on the floor, against the stacks, and cried. *I can never love.*

I gained fifty pounds in four months. I lost friends, skipped school, quit playing tennis, and covered it all up with lies. My twin brother, on the other hand, made the honor roll and the basketball team. I offered hair-trigger sarcasm.

"No one knows how to talk to you anymore," my mother would say.

"Then don't," I snapped.

By the time senior year rolled around, I had blocked out that day in the library from my conscious memory. I was smoking pot and I had skipped so much school that even with decent grades they said I couldn't graduate. How could I have been so stupid?

With my parents angry, I hid in my room and read. I discovered the story of the phoenix, the mythological bird that sets itself on fire and from the ruins of its own ashes, rises to live again. Mythology gave me hope. I felt an allegorical kinship. I knew the symbolism of the phoenix rising story would influence the rest of my life, and I knew it was a good omen because it would guide me. If I wanted to live with integrity, I had to accept, to my unending regret, that I'd set the fire myself. But I could learn resilience and rise from the ashes of my own mistakes.

Finally, in college, I saw a psychiatrist. With his help I was able to understand the roots of my deep depression—that I was a good person who also happened to be gay.

"I'm not surprised," my mother said when I told her, "but I would like to think this over before we speak further." She cried, but not because I was gay. "My concern," she said the next day, "is that the world will be harsher toward you than my other children."

After she told my father, he said, "She's still my daughter and I love her." He died a few months later, the two of us having never spoken about it.

My sister died a year later, and I worried about my mother. They'd been very close, and I knew that I couldn't take my sister's place.

I'd been scraping by cleaning houses and desperately wanting a grown-up job in my field. One day, my mother stopped by my apartment for lunch and found me in a fury. I blamed my anger on what I believed to be the necessity of hiding my gay identity at a job interview I had the following morning. "There's no place for the real me," I cried to her.

My mother tried to help. "Interview, get the job, and then come out later," she said, with her customary pragmatism.

"You don't understand. I can't pretend anymore." Words were trapped inside me. I'd always had intuitions about people, knew things about people that they often didn't know about themselves. I paid an emotional price for that skill.

All of a sudden, Nancy, the child, started a fight. "You don't care."

"Pumpkin," she said, "what's wrong?"

We yelled back and forth. I told her that the world doesn't want me. I could see that she was trying to understand, but she couldn't, because I'm having the real conversation in my head.

I am not your Pumpkin, I was crying. I knew I shouldn't be speaking to my mother like this. My thoughts raced. A mother can't be all things to all children. My mother is a good person. My mother is deeply flawed. My mother hides her feelings. My mother loves her children. My mother is standing in my living room, in her raincoat, trying to help me. I was pacing to the window and back. *I'm a failure. Because I can't cross the divide into the adult world. Because I'm gay in a straight world. Because, because, because . . .*

"And if we're really being honest, let's face it," I said, bursting with suicidal insight. "If you had to lose a daughter, we both know who you'd choose."

My mother didn't make a move. She was in no hurry. Her

hazel eyes, the color of rain, looked out at me. She was still standing. Her shoulders softened. Regret anchored her in place, not because what I said wasn't true, but because she didn't want me to feel unwanted, unloved. Her gaze never wavered from me. She was standing for me. After all the years I'd spent running from her, my mother was shocked to discover that I wanted a real relationship with her.

For the first time, I understood her perspective; she'd lost the one daughter that had cared about her. She had felt rejected by me.

Just then my two cats raced each other into the living room. Aries, the calico, always took the lead. Rosie, the orange tabby, was a bit of a bumbler. Their arrival seemed almost festive. It was good timing, too, because I didn't know what else to say, or how to thank my mother for not ducking from the bomb blast.

Rosie slipped on the wooden floor while making a sharp right, following her sister up onto the couch. I chuckled, because it was typical Rosie. Then a spark of pleasure catapulted into understanding. I got it. My spirits soared. I totally got it.

"I love both my cats," I said, spontaneously, "but Aries is my favorite."

"She is?" My mother looked over at the cat and back at me.

"She's a troublemaker like I am." I sat down on the couch and Rosie found my lap. "She's a little klutzy," I said, waving her paw in the air.

My mother nodded, she understood; we were all right.

I don't know what happened after that. Maybe a leaf fell off a tree, the phone rang, or I went to get dressed. We went to lunch. The next day, I got the job.

For the rest of her life—ten years—my mother referred to me as her best friend. She shared her gambling follies, her stock market predictions, and her opinions—unsolicited—on anything and everything. If she liked something, she assumed, or at least hoped, that I'd like it, too. I got hooked on the soap opera *Dallas* because of my mother. We went to the movies, took long drives, and picked out beautiful homes we would have liked to live in someday.

She didn't like cats, but Zak got high marks. During one particularly aggressive thunderstorm, she called to ask me if he was in or out. "I opened the front door for him," I told her, "but he doesn't need a weatherman to know which way the hail falls."

My mother took pleasure in watching her children mature, and in turn, I had the extraordinary experience of getting to know her softer side, the one she hid behind her stoicism. No longer wary of being hurt by me she shared her loneliness, her hidden dreams, and the unshakable depth of her love for her siblings, even when they hurt her.

Many of my clients hunger for more closeness with their parents. "Sometimes it's possible," I tell them. "But the first step is accepting that people who love each other hurt each other. After that, you have to stop reacting to it the way you did as a child."

It's not easy. My mother was forever saying, "Nancy, can you please wear a little lipstick?" "Can you cancel your clients and meet me at the beach?" "I think you should get back with so-and-so." Instead of getting annoyed, I'd make a joke.

But I hounded her, too. "Did you make your doctor's appointment?" "Are you still gambling?" "There's only junk food in the fridge!"

In the months after my mother's death, I'd wake up and stare out the kitchen window. I was inconsolable. I was afraid I'd have only static memories of her while I continued to grow and change. But words she'd spoken and experiences we'd shared continued to feel dynamic and relevant. I discovered I liked lipstick a little bit too late for her to enjoy, but sometimes when I put it on I think, "Mom, you'd be so proud."

Valerie was only six months old when my mother died, but Tori's disappearance had unexpectedly forged a link between them in my memories; the shape of love, then and now. Engaging in repair is a form of love too. The myth of the phoenix rising has served me well. Condemned at fourteen of being "incapable of loving," I've worked all my life to lift the curse. To my lament, each relationship—partner, friend, family, and pet—creates a fear specific to that relationship. As an adult, I know that my fears are ancient and irrational, and that most people struggle to love well. But the ghost of that girl still wanders. Years later, before my poster odyssey ended, she found me again.

HAVE YOU SEEN OUR CAT?

$1,000 REWARD!

Help us find 'Shelby.' 7 YO Female. De-clawed front paws. Loud meower.
Reward for her safe return. No questions asked.
We're heartbroken as is our 4-year-old son. Please help.

Please call (212) 555-6192.

SHELBY

I was an uncaffeinated therapist dragging herself to work, and I was supposed to be preparing a big to-do list for our new apartment in Manhattan. Karis had enrolled at New York University. I was relieved by her decision. Six years earlier, before we'd met, I'd begun practicing psychotherapy in the city, two days a week. I'd stay one night in my good friend's spare room/office; the next day after work I'd take a late train back to New Haven. That way I had the best of both worlds: the exciting cultural offerings of New York and the more restful pace of living in Connecticut. After Karis moved in, I continued my routine.

About the time Karis bumped into her thirtieth birthday, she decided to major in social work, fearing that studying English literature would prepare her only for unemployment. We'd been together for two years at that point. Her decision to study at NYU took some pressure off us and added others. We rented a beautiful sunny studio in Chelsea slightly bigger than a Volkswagen, and kept the house in New Haven. Some days we never saw each other because we were in opposite cities. One of us had to check on Zak and the house. New York was out of the question for him. He'd be miserable with an apartment window that opened onto the fire escape.

We loved living in New York, but our tight quarters posed new relationship challenges. When I wanted to feel as if I were alone, I stood in the galley kitchen with my back to Karis and read *Vanity Fair*. She zoned out by playing spider solitaire on the computer. Separately we each took a lot of hot baths, locking the door for an added sense of privacy. We concentrated on learning the etiquette of apartment living. What is acceptable to wear at night when you're bringing your garbage to the trash chute next to the elevator? Are pajamas okay? Is a bathrobe more dignified? Babydoll lingerie, as worn by the lady down the hall, was a definite *no*.

I was on my way to the hardware store when I'd been dazzled by my latest discovery. "Shelby is a perfect poster," I said, talking to myself in the midst of New York's rush hour traffic. And then I corrected myself. "What sort of person is happy to discover a lost-cat poster?" A fleeting image came to mind—Golem, in *The Lord of the Rings*. I was swiping a lost-cat poster from a crosswalk pole and thinking, *My precious.*

If I was handing out blue ribbons, Shelby should win for best design. The photographs were of outstanding quality, and both the graphics and the message completely drew me in. HAVE YOU SEEN OUR CAT? It didn't seem like a public announcement. Rather, the owners were personally asking me for help, and since they were asking so nicely, I desperately wanted to find seven-year-old adorable Shelby, the "loud meower."

The photograph on the left side of the poster captured a classic cat moment—kitty caught playing in the clothes dryer. The picture on the right showed her in partial repose, leg extended, displaying a smooth, pink paw pad that never touched the gritty outdoors. Shelby was an easy guess: sheltered, indoor city cat. Her owners, I assumed, were connected to fashion, advertising, or the art world.

Visually, the poster was a winner, but the text read more like an SOS. She'd disappeared yesterday. A $1,000 reward, marked in red and black, commanded the viewer's attention. But even more striking than the money were the phrases "Reward for her safe return," and "No questions asked." Shelby's disappearance was not an accident. The family was offering the returnee a guarantee of safe passage by disguising a ransom as a reward. Would it motivate the bad guys, or at least a secondary player, to produce Shelby?

In the Nancy Drew mysteries, Shelby's family would try to hire her as a private detective. But after scanning the lost-cat poster, Nancy would look up and say, "I'll help for free." Their tear-stained, four-year-old son would say, "Please find her," while the mother offered an encouraging smile. But this wasn't fiction. This was the modern urban jungle and Shelby's family had to do the legwork themselves.

Some people might choke at the idea of a $1,000 reward, but I'm sure that a lot of pet owners, if they could afford it, would spend a similar sum. Nevertheless, I wasn't sure about the over-all viability of rewards. Do they really motivate the public to search for a missing cat? Don't pet lovers search because they feel for the owner? Lost-cat Web sites encourage the use of rewards, but I think that in the same way that posters provide owners with a sense of comfort and a semblance of control, a reward holds out a bet on a brighter future. At least money (so the thinking goes) will keep the public engaged in searching for my cat.

But the public has a complicated response to rewards. One day, a woman sitting next to me on the train snuck a peek at my laptop screen and asked me what I did for a living. Her thrusting chin bothered me. "I'm a writer, cats," I said, thinking it was a morsel of incidental information. She immediately launched into a story about a neighboring family who'd offered a $5,000 reward for their missing cat.

"That's disgusting," she told me. "I called up the mother and told her that she was teaching her kids the wrong values and that

she should use the money to feed the poor. Or give it to charity."
The woman stared into my eyes, the way the self-righteous do
when demanding validation. I stared at her diamond rings.

I finally spoke with Shelby's owners at the end of what I refer
to as a "theme day at work." A theme day can be identified only
after it's unfolded, when I realize that I've been hearing the
same thing from different people. "I wish I had more friends,"
"I forgot to bring my checkbook," and "I'm sick of therapy" are
popular topics.

That day's theme was the hassle of finding a decent apartment. ("Cockroaches wouldn't rent the apartment I saw." "It
was a closet with a refrigerator and stove inside it." "It was a
great apartment . . . over a karaoke bar.") I offered empathy. I'd
found my own apartment only by word of mouth and I'd been
given twenty minutes to make my decision.

I had waited a month to call Shelby's owners, hoping her
family had had a chance to find her. Little did I know that my
theme day would continue. Shelby, it seemed, had disappeared
from a locked apartment. "We're the only ones who have a key,"
Jackie told me when we spoke, referring to her husband and her
son. "Absolutely."

But the crime scene was puzzling. There were no signs of
forced entry. Surely someone *had* to have used a key. But they'd
never given one out to a neighbor. In fact, they'd never even had
an extra set made. It was the family's custom to leave Shelby
plenty of food and water whenever they went out of town, rather
than enlist a neighbor to help. "This is Manhattan," Jackie said
wryly. "We were cordial, not close." It was too late for a "meet-
the-neighbors-wine-and-cheese-and-did-you-steal-my-cat" reception.

I was on Jackie's team. My identity radiated "I live in New
York, too." My keyless neighbor had once knocked on our door
at midnight and climbed out of our window onto the fire escape
before shimmying into her apartment. I received my guest wear-

ing a ratty T-shirt and gym pants. (Karis was wearing flannel pajamas covered with ducks.) A week later, I bumped into that same neighbor in the elevator. I said hello. She nodded while staring at the buttons on the wall like they were central to unraveling the Da Vinci Code. I looked down at my cowboy boots and searched the leather stitching for an answer. Did I fail in pajamas or personality? I eagerly anticipated my next opportunity, when I could leave her knocks unanswered. I'd find her the following morning; I fantasized, lying in the hallway, facedown on her Prada handbag.

"Shelby's disappearance seemed unbelievable," Jackie said. "Even implausible." The family had gone out of town for two days over the Thanksgiving break, and were looking forward to Shelby's homecoming ritual of running to the door and rubbing up against her family's legs.

They took the elevator to their third-floor loft. The elevator was designed so that instead of pushing a button to get to the floor you wanted, you inserted a key into the wall panel. Each keyhole corresponded to a specific floor, and the door opened only on the floor that had been keyed. The family's loft spanned the entire third floor, so when the elevator opened, it opened directly into their home. "We were joking about whose legs she'd rub against first, but when we got home, there was no Shelby. Anywhere!"

Curious at first, the family members each took off in a different direction to check out Shelby's favorite sleeping spots. Once they'd covered those, they invented new ones. When futility finally set in, they changed course and searched for an explanation.

"The elevator is our security system, too," Jackie's words hovered with suspense. "Maybe somebody broke in." Although the loft had several windows and a back door, they remained locked from the inside. "You can imagine, we were desperate to find Shelby, but we were scared, too. How did someone get in? We searched everywhere to see what else was missing. In drawers, in closets, in all those places, nothing was stolen—except Shelby!"

Jackie had a lovely voice, full of inflection, intelligence, and feeling. Her words fell easily into place. They weren't tied up in the sorrow of long-standing emotional conflict. No fear, no hesitancy, no moods. Jackie had a voice that threw back the covers and wanted to get out of bed in the morning. I knew without meeting her that she was beautiful.

She and her family began knocking on their neighbors' doors. Had anyone seen Shelby? Had they been burglarized? Had any other strange events occurred in the building? They seemed like simple questions.

Often the couple's queries were greeted with the disclaimer: "I'm not a cat person," as if that explained everything. As the conversations continued, the couple grew restless, but they fought the urge to step away. They might glean a scrap of relevant information, if only they could figure out whom to believe. Shelby had been here or there or nowhere at all. "Everyone acted like it was classified information," Jackie said, baffled. "We just wanted our cat."

Finally, one woman spilled a few beans. Over the holiday, someone (who wanted to remain anonymous) had called the building's elevator repairman without informing any of the other tenants. The couple pieced together a theory. Working from the basement, but never actually traveling in the elevator itself, the repairman had apparently opened and closed the elevator door on each floor. For Shelby, the elevator's ascension was the urban version of a trumpet heralding her family's return. The trio of grunts, groans, and squeaks never failed to rouse the sleeping cat. Cued to her family's impending presence, Shelby would run to the elevator door and wait for it to open. This time, however, the car would have been empty when it reached Shelby's floor. It would still have sparked her ritual, though, and when the door opened, she probably scooted inside. The door must have closed before she could get out.

A disoriented Shelby probably didn't exit until the doors opened on the top floor. Jackie knocked on someone's fifth-floor apartment door. The man who lived there had pawned Shelby off on another fifth-floor neighbor, but she was going downtown. "Downtown" then tossed her into a rehearsal hall with a troupe of dancers on the fourth floor (the building being a combination of residential and commercial spaces).

Jackie went to the studio and listened to the dancers speed through a no-frills recap of the events she'd already heard about, but then they added a new chapter.

"They said the stray jumped out of the fourth-story window," she told me, incredulous. "And when they ran down to the street, they couldn't find her."

I felt tears rush to the back of my eyes. I was afraid to hear the rest of the story. Although she was shocked by the news, Jackie tried to coordinate her thoughts. Usually a synopsis like the one the dancers provided simplifies your understanding of facts and clarifies a chain of events. That leads to this and this leads to that. But Shelby was a timid cat. She wouldn't sit on a ledge in front of an open window during the chaos of a dance rehearsal, much less leap into an abyss.

"Unfathomable," Jackie declared. "It's simply unbelievable. They knew she wasn't a stray. She looks like an indoor cat. She's healthy and declawed. And somehow they couldn't locate an indoor cat after she dropped four stories and landed on the sidewalk?"

The possibilities were alarming. Did Jackie mean that the dancers had simply thrown Shelby out the window? Or that she'd fallen to the street and disappeared? Or that the dancers never even went to look for Shelby? "The dancers put her out on the street," Jackie said. "In the cold. At night. On Thanksgiving!"

Subsequently, Jackie obliterated the dancers' account to its fictional core. She interviewed shopkeepers and friends who worked or lived on her block and learned that on the day of Shelby's disappearance, people had heard a cat meowing for three hours. Despite her disappointment, Jackie understood their reluctance to get involved. "They couldn't have known, particularly in New York City, whether the cat was feral or someone's missing pet," she said.

You can't help but wonder, what's up with the neighbors in Jackie's building? They ranged from polite to indifferent to callous. Whether the lack of cohesion was due to conflict with the management company, the landlord, other residents, or even an inability to overcome the building's culture, for whatever reason, the neighbors prized their aloofness. Somehow, without leadership, trust, open communication, accountability, or a feeling of group belonging, people lived in this expensive building. "We were cordial," Jackie had said. She and her husband were part of the system, too.

These people couldn't suspend their individual desires, even for a few hours, in order to work together to solve the task of handling a stray. It was becoming clear to me why the decision to call the elevator repairman had to remain a dirty little secret. Any one decision by an individual could be co-opted by the neighbors for target practice on scapegoating night.

Had this always been the culture in the building? Or had there been a recent change? "I knew there were personality differences," Jackie said.

"Nice euphemism," I teased. "Here's my interpretation: 'I can't stand your guts.'" After a few years of experience, I'd become more bold as a sleuth. Reality beckoned—Jackie's neighbors played rough.

I heard a diminutive laugh, and then she said, "I guess it was more serious than I'd realized."

At this point, I thought I should expand my scope of inquiry.

Did Shelby live in an ethical sinkhole? Or was the building's culture considered normal for New York? Despite my haughty next-door neighbor, the suffocating heat in the winter, and a capricious elevator, I loved the building where I lived. Most of my neighbors were friendly, but the few who weren't were at least interesting. I planned on asking some friends, lifelong New Yorkers, to describe the culture in their apartment buildings: *Breakfast at Tiffany's* or *Rear Window*? Circle one. In Jackie's building, it had taken only a few hours to white-out Shelby's seven-year-old identity from family pet to stray.

The family used heavy packing tape to hang Shelby's posters. Swathing each one around a pole or a mailbox, they labored for ten long crosstown blocks from the East Side to the West Side.

"There were two posters," I said. "One of them looked Arabic or Hebrew. What were the swirls underneath Shelby's photographs?"

"My son wanted to help," Jackie answered tenderly. "He's four."

A few hours later, after they'd hung the very last poster, the phone rang and a friend of Jackie's offered her a suggestion. She should consult an "urban animal tracker." Jackie had never heard of such a thing. Neither had I.

Richard lived in Greenwich Village, and the title Urban Animal Tracker was his invention. He tracked the wildlife movement in Central Park such as raccoons, foxes, turtles, and an occasional lost coyote. He also helped people looking for their missing pets in the city. He was the intermediary Jackie needed, the twenty-first-century, iconoclastic, urban gumshoe.

Upon receiving Jackie's call, Richard immediately took a cab uptown and showed the family how to search for Shelby. Using a piece of clothing that had her scent on it, he traced what he imagined were her possible hiding spots. Among other places, he checked crates, frozen garbage bags, exposed pipes, gratings, and even cracks in the outside of the building. They left behind some of her favorite dry food. "He stayed for hours," Jackie said, "and he was wonderful, refusing to let us pay him. We were grateful, but we still couldn't find her."

City life hustled on the street below, while the family limped along without Shelby. Then, five days after Shelby disappeared, a stranger intervened. Jackie referred to him as "the Gentleman." The Gentlemen had been visiting with "his buddies," musicians who jammed in a recording studio around the corner from Jackie's loft. Earlier in the week, they had discovered a cat sitting on the sidewalk, just outside the door to the studio. Believing it to be the landlord's cat, the musicians rescued her from the cold.

One night, while walking over to the studio, the Gentleman stopped to read a lost-cat poster. When he arrived at the studio he had a feeling that his friends had rescued Shelby. But the cat had remained in hiding, and the musicians' memories were vague. It had a mix of colors. The Gentleman wanted them to see the poster, so he grabbed his jacket again and went out to find one.

A few minutes later, he returned with the poster. Their rescued cat was indeed Shelby! After the Gentleman's phone call, Jackie grabbed a box of dry food and literally ran over to the studio. "I rattled the box just like we do at home, but no Shelby," she said. She continued to explore the studio with The Gentleman at her side, but figuring that Shelby might be afraid of him, he left and waited outside. Soon after, Shelby pink-nosed her way out from underneath a curtain.

Shelby's life returned to its former glory. She'd retained her sweet temperament, and her only change in behavior was to faithfully join the four-year-old son in bed every night instead of intermittently, as she'd done in the past. No more sleeping at the end of the bed, Shelby purred on top of the pillow. Not unusual news. Most of the owners reported that their cats went back to their old routines. A few of the very old indoor cats were no longer running to the door looking for adventure. They'd seen the other side and it didn't include a food bowl.

Jackie was ecstatic to have Shelby home, but her disillusionment lingered. She took the cat to the vet for a post-escape checkup. The vet's diagnosis was the death knell to the dancers' lies. When a cat drops from a four-story building and lands on the sidewalk, you'd expect to find some scrapes or broken bones, or possibly a broken jaw. The vet was almost certain Shelby hadn't fallen—she had only one small cut on her ear, probably from a scuffle with the *real* studio cat.

"I just don't understand. The dancers just put Shelby out on the street, and the neighbors didn't care," she moaned. "Five days of grief. What happened to kindness?"

It was the $64 million question: How did so many people fail to act with kindness? Jackie's question presupposed that kindness exists, but that it had failed to appear in Shelby's case. Her point of view, according to the emerging science of empathy, is accurate. We know that aggression is innate, but it appears that kindness is innate, too. People feel good when they help others. After only eighteen months, a toddler will offer to help an adult she doesn't know in picking up a dropped object. By age three, children are more generous to a child who's already treated them with kindness.

How then does an innate tendency become compromised? One theory posits that as you grow older you must choose between your needs and the needs of others, and that creates inner conflict. If only it were that simple. Empathy research has also found that along with the development of kindness beginning at age three, group identification begins to form. Life becomes a balance between you, me, and my group values. Moral dilemmas stem from the inevitable differences among them.

But empathy, I believe, is part of our moral obligation. Randy Cohen, "The Ethicist," wrote in one of his *New York Times*

Magazine columns, "If you had taken in a cat some stranger left at your back door, you couldn't then simply abandon it by the side of the road. Some obligations we gain inadvertently."*

Empathy became less and less available for Shelby each time she was passed along—by the fourth or fifth person, the story had probably lost context and coherence. "It's a lost cat. A stray. Never saw him before. I don't think he lives in the building."

But the dancers knew that they were avoiding not only empathy, but a moral obligation, too. How can I be so sure? If it had been morally justifiable to put a stray cat out on the street, then there would have been no need to create a group lie about it. One lie wasn't enough. It begat two. And no one deviated from the lies, either.

I tried to cheer Jackie up, mentioning that strangers like Richard and the Gentleman had more than enough kindness to make up for the drought in her building. I also shared my anecdotal experiences. In the stories I'd heard, rescuers, whether they were cat lovers or not, had refused to accept money in return for finding someone's missing pet. They wouldn't even consider it. "That gives me faith in human nature," she said.

"Shelby's lost-cat poster won grand prize for design," I told her. "The message is clear. The graphics are great, and the photos are perfectly charming."

"My husband is in graphics," Jackie laughed. "He'll be proud."

A few days later, I met my friend Russell at a café. Russell is a generous man who owns the Avalon Salon in the West Village. We began talking about cats. "I'm not a cat person," he announced, as if I suffered from amnesia. He takes his Shih Tzu to work every day. "If I saw a strange cat in my elevator, I probably wouldn't get in."

* http://www.nytimes.com/2009/11/22/magazine/22FOB-ethicist-t .html

I swallowed the bait. "Why?"

"Because it could maul me to death."

"You're an adult, right?"

"Okay, maybe that's an exaggeration," he conceded, "but I don't know this cat. I have no clue if it's declawed. I'm not going to check its claws. It might scratch me. I don't want to get involved. I'm not a cat person."

How many times have I heard this declaration? "I'm not a cat person." It seemed like a catchall phrase to avoid responsibility. How many types of "I'm not a cat person are there"?

Type A: "I'm not fond of two- and four-legged life forms."

Type B: "I'm not an animal person."

Type C: "Hate cats, too spooky."

Type D: "I'm a dog person (nose in the air)."

All four categories offered a free pass to the moral fuzzy zone. I could see the advantages of such self-proclamations.

"Did you find a briefcase in the elevator?"

"I'm not a briefcase person."

"Did you help the man having a heart attack in the elevator?"

"I'm not a heart attack person."

"What did you do with the gold left in the elevator?"

"The stray gold? I gave it to my neighbor. He was going downtown so he gave it to someone else. She's not a gold person, either. She gave it to some dancers. They put the gold on the ledge, but not being good with heights, it fell out of the fourth-floor window. They ran downstairs, but couldn't find a trace of it."

"Wouldn't you at least put a sign up in the lobby?" I asked Russell.

He nodded, yes, of course.

"What would you do if you saw a little mutt in the elevator?"

"Well, that's a different story," Russell said. "You *know* the dog is lost!"

I asked one more non-cat person whom I still respected, a Brooklyn native who lives in a co-op building. "I have allergies," she said, "but I'd leave the cat in the lobby with a bowl of food. If it was a holiday weekend when normal schedules are crazy, the cat has a better chance of being rescued if people coming into the building can see it. Or I'd at least put up a lost-cat poster. Or call the management company and report a found cat." She took a breath and said: "There's something wrong with Jackie's building. She should move."

What brought Shelby home? Altruism and kindness. Not the reward. At the end of the day, responding to a lost cat is an act of generosity and empathy toward other human beings. Labels such as "cat person" and "dog person" miss the mark entirely. Who brought Shelby home? If we're slinging around labels, a "people person," is a befitting description. Someone who cared about Jackie and her family. Someone who didn't live in the building, whose hardwiring hadn't atrophied from years of stale, group norms. An outsider. Just like in the movies, a stranger came to town and cleaned up the neighborhood by acting on his own moral standards. He wears a white hat. We never learn his name. He's simply remembered as "the Gentleman."

Missing Cat

White & Black, Hairy, Male, No Collar.

Call: (272) 555 3164

Reward!

MAOMY

The description of the missing cat included four heavy hitters: "white," "black," "male," and "no collar." Check, check, check, check. The fifth word was . . . "hairy"? "Hairy" does not get a check. Ever.

Nancy Drew read the poster twice, and then a third time. I scanned the street, the parked cars, the houses, the sidewalks, and the telephone pole with the poster tacked to it. Everything looked normal. And yet, I wondered if I'd unknowingly entered an alternate universe, where all the other cats were hairless and this hairy one stood out. Who thought "hairy" was a good idea? Even a child, I reasoned, would be more likely to use "furry."

And then it hit me. This was after all New Haven, The bare text, and ironic tone screamed young and male. Probably some Yale fraternity guys imitating David Letterman's Top Ten list had made it into a game. In fact, I could picture it. During a blowout keg party, they'd lost the house cat. "How do you describe a missing cat?" The winner: "Hairy."

These guys were most likely being funny, although many well-intentioned folks often make mistakes when creating lost-cat posters. Many owners forget to include essential descriptors, such as coloring, gender, appearance, and personality traits.

This poster, for example, lacked the fundamentals: date, time, and location of the disappearance.

Then there are the cat owners occupying the other end of the spectrum who include incidental information. These obsessives describe their cat by weight, including ounces. Unless the cat is anorexic or too fat to tie its shoelaces, poundage can be misleading. Besides, if I capture a stray, I won't be putting it on a scale. Obsessives also write descriptors such as: "Doesn't like other cats," "Please approach Fluffy quietly, she's shy," and "Scared of loud voices."

But a poster can include each and every one of the vital criteria and still undermine the owner's good intentions if it becomes outdated and ravaged by time. Owners often fail to anticipate how quickly we, the public, can turn fatalistic and stop looking for a cat we think is long gone. It's best for cats owners to put up new posters with new dates, or at least add "still missing" along the bottom of the original.

Maomy's poster was in good shape, though, which meant it had only been facing the elements for a few days. February hadn't had time to beat it off the pole. I looked forward to a lively conversation with the owners, filled with sophomoric witticisms. College kids were like that.

It's a good thing I didn't bet the farm.

"Do you know where he is?" Kim asked when I called. "Did you find my cat?" Earlier that afternoon she and her young son had driven through the neighborhood, hanging more posters. She'd made her first set two months earlier, but the bitter winter had torn through them.

At first, I thought she didn't understand the purpose of my call, so I tried to clarify. She waited through my explanation, and when I finished, she asked, "Do you think I can find my cat?" She had dreamt that she'd found him the night before and wanted to know if I thought the dream was a sign. She thought it was.

Her plaintive questions hung in the air. "Do you think he will come back?" I've spoken with many distressed owners, but Kim was the only one who asked for a prognosis. I was scrounging around for something substantial to say, something beyond mere platitudes. Then she asked me if I believed that dreams could be a sign.

I happen to love dream interpretation, although I'm careful not to impose a meaning onto someone else's imagination. A dream may be a premonition, but I'm reluctant to assume that's the case. Dreams can also be an emotional substitute for the realities of life. They can be an illumination of unconscious feelings that need attention and a connection to the basic human archetypes that make up our psyche, such as the warrior, the mother, and the mystic.

I once encountered a series of dreams over a four-year period that provided me with an ongoing progress report for a client of mine who'd remained in a relationship where she felt devalued by her boyfriend. During our first session, Faith—who was young, single, and childless—shared a disturbing nightmare. She'd thrown a baby off a bridge and watched it drown. We both interpreted the dream as a symbol of her decimated emotional self. She hated her vulnerability and felt unable to take care of her own needs.

In the second year of therapy, she dreamt that she was nine months pregnant, but couldn't give birth. In the third year, she gave birth, but couldn't find the baby afterward. A hallmark dream occurred during the fourth and final year of therapy, in which she became the parent of a three-year-old girl. Shortly thereafter, Faith ended her demoralizing relationship. "I respect myself too much to stay with him."

"I believe in dreams, sometimes," I said to Kim. "What do you believe?"

"Sometimes," she answered and fell silent.

"Did anyone call after seeing your posters?"

"Only once," she said. "It looked like my cat, but it wasn't." Explaining that *Maomy* was Chinese for cat, Kim said that it sounded like the name "Mimi." My mispronunciation elicited a chuckle. Maomy was five years old.

I discovered that Kim fit into the disadvantaged category of cat owners who punch a time clock. One day, Kim's roommate called her at work. The cat was missing! The roommate and her boyfriend weren't sure how it'd happened. Of course, Kim wanted to start searching for Maomy immediately, but she was a doctor in residency and was locked into a mandatory thirty-six-hour shift at Yale-New Haven Hospital. She asked her fellow residents for help. "Please, could someone switch their schedule?" But it wasn't a death in the family; it was only a cat. They reassured her, "He'll come back."

As tired as she was when she got off her shift, she typed out a poster, copied it, and taped it all over the neighborhood, then searched for an hour before getting some sleep. She went to bed feeling frustrated and disappointed. A day later, her feelings had changed. A few details had come to light.

Her roommate's boyfriend had ignored the apartment's no-smoking rule. While sneaking a cigarette in the kitchen, he opened the back door to clear the air and watched Maomy, an indoor cat, scamper into the night. Eventually, like a dead body stuffed into the trunk of a car, the boyfriend's secret had to be dumped. When his girlfriend couldn't shake her guilt over losing Maomy, he finally confessed to her, and she relayed the revised edition of the truth. "I could live with an accident, but he was a coward," Kim said, each word spoken with contempt. "Where was the respect? Where?"

The obstacles mounted. Her lease had ended a month after Maomy's disappearance, and she'd had to move to another apartment, but on her days off, Kim returned to her old neighborhood and continued the search, hoping he might still be nearby.

On one prior occasion, Maomy had slipped out the door and jumped over the fence. About ten seconds later, he'd reversed direction and jumped back. Kim was holding out that it might happen again.

Some researchers believe that cats travel only a few houses away and then hide simply because they're scared. In time, their scent recirculates in the new location until it becomes familiar, and their hiding place begins to feel like their home. So even after their owners call to them by name, their instincts—command central—override the value of human relationships, and they remain undercover.

Strategies should vary when searching for an indoor cat versus an outdoor cat. For a missing outdoor cat, it makes sense to wonder: Is he stuck, injured, or dead? But for a missing indoor cat who has disappeared out of doors, pursue this question: Where is the nearest place that he would hide?

"Should I still put up pictures and advertise?" Kim asked me, her focus returning to what mattered to her the most. She had been searching in her neighborhood for a month. Now, her instincts were locked in a battle between longing and pragmatism. Longing was fueling her determination, but she was trapped between two fears. Was she being realistic or giving up prematurely? "Is it too late?"

I looked out my window at the dirty snow piled by the road. Between the gray trees, the wind, and the fact that it was black as night when it was supposed to be afternoon, I wasn't sensing that this timid indoor cat had survived a February freeze. During our conversation, I came to doubt that Maomy had been taken in by a Good Samaritan. But I wasn't going to send Kim in a direction she wasn't ready to follow. I thought I was calling to hear about the story that had already happened, but she was expanding my role and I wanted to be sensitive in the third act.

My training as a therapist took over.

Timing in therapy is delicate, and although Kim wasn't a client, I could see that she was grappling with her heart and mind. *But sometimes a miracle can occur.*

"Maybe someone took him in?" I said without conviction.

Kim paused. And paused some more. I didn't rush to fill the silence. The pause became a statement. Maybe she had nothing more to say. Was my silence helpful or making her uncomfortable? Had I overstepped my bounds? I hadn't anticipated guiding a lost-cat owner to an emotional resolution.

Then about twenty long seconds later, she ended her silence, the tension lifting as she spoke. "He is dead," she said.

It wasn't a question. It wasn't directed at me. She said it for herself. "He was a sweet, at-home cat," she said. "He likes to sit near you. He didn't like to be held."

It was the hallmark of a new mourner—Kim was alternating between using past and present tenses. "He'd sit on my desk," she said, reminiscing a little more, "and I'd study." For the moment, she seemed peaceful. "He was funny," she said, followed by a pause. She'd put the eulogy on hold.

To those coping with grief, whether they're recovering from a breakup or the death of a loved one or even a natural disaster, I always say that you need to live through a minimum of four seasons, because memories will be activated by traditions. Some clients hate my forecast. Others find it liberating—now they aren't crazy just because they crave and need more time to heal.

Who has the right to say how long it takes to grieve?

"It's been two years since your sister died," my mother told me one day. "Every day, I've taken her photo album out of the drawer, had a good cry, and then put it back. Today I put the album away for good. I stopped rereading the postcards she sent from Europe. It's time to stop mourning. Time to live in the present. I feel good today," she said while tying her sneakers. "My joints don't hurt. I could walk to the moon."

Her newfound lightness unburdened an ancient grief. Six

months after my grandmother had died (I was ten years old), my mother went to the bank to close the estate. She maintained her composure until she walked outside of the building. Then she became dizzy and leaned against the wall. "I looked at the envelope in my hand," she said, "and thought, I don't want money—I want my mother back."

Grief is like that. Dormant and alive all at once. Grief can also be a tribute. As with Kim's celebration of her cat, the loss of a loved one can be mitigated by the joy we feel about who they were. In death, remembering the quirks of our loved ones makes their presence more real. My mother and I used to argue because she didn't believe in an afterlife, "When you're in the dirt," she used to say, "that's it! Just dust."

"Very poetic," I said, teasing her. "You undercut the sages and the mystics." But I found proof, well, my version of it, while on the cat-poster trail, many years after I spoke with Kim. I'd never forgotten her exquisite moment of recognition when she felt Maomy's dual presence—here and gone.

Kim began to experience multiple layers of sadness, including the anticipation of helping her son say good-bye. "My son misses the cat," she said. At night, Maomy liked to sit on the sink while her son took a bath. I wished her peace in the coming months. "Thank you for calling," Kim said sweetly. "That was kind of you." After a pause, she said: "Maomy likes cucumbers."

MY CAT SYDNEY IS LOST

she is a calico

alot of white and orange and some black

5.5 yrs old - thin - very beautiful

missing since noon

on Tuesday January 2nd

she lives on Orange Street

with Liz and Buster the dog, along with 3 cats

who miss her very much

if you see her or have her please call (415) 555-7611

SYDNEY

It was a rotten day to lose your cat. The snow began as a soft fall of powder, but by late afternoon it was icy and hard. I prepared for the storm by driving to the laundromat to pick up my warm clothes. When I stepped out of the car, I saw a parade of yellow lost-cat posters tacked up on every telephone pole and every tree, on each of the four streets that led away from the intersection. Each seemingly dusted by brush strokes of white.

I could tell that I had a motivated and detail-oriented owner on my hands. She'd listed her first and last name, full address, and telephone number. I ruled out "shy." Her unusual heading, MY CAT SYDNEY IS LOST, expressed not only the facts, but the attitude as well. She was emphasizing that Sydney was *her* cat (5.5 years together), and not just any ol' missing cat. This is Sydney we're talking about!

Overall, Anne seemed to be very strong willed, a real go-getter. There was something perfectly confident about her actions. She'd taken the liberty of being the spokesperson for her dog, Buster, and her three other cats, as well. They "miss her very much." Was it true, or just wishful thinking? Short of a condolence card, how could she tell? Maybe they were happy to have one less mouth crowding the feed bowl (and more legroom, too). According to the poster, Sydney had dashed outdoors at high noon. I wasn't downcast about her prospects. Instead of devouring Sydney, maybe the storm would chase her home. I conjured a gripping television drama. Liz's poster portrayed a strong family unit—Buster and the three sibling cats were right by her side, mourning Sydney's disappearance. My show would be a mini version of *Storm Stories*, but instead of rescue teams tracking lost hikers, we'd see Liz and her dog as they scoured the neighborhood, searching for Sydney. Her other cats would be waiting at home, anxiously shredding the sofa while a media circus tented up on the sidewalk. Photographers would elbow one another trying to get the best shots through the living room window. For the cliffhanger, the sheriff would turn to the camera and say, "Time is running out. By nightfall, the temperature will drop into the single digits."

My show ended up having a season-long run. I was able to monitor Liz's search simply by looking out the window as I went back and forth to the Wash Hut every week. Seven days later, I saw duplicate posters in purple hanging on additional streets, while the original yellow posters remained at full force. By the third week, it was a rainbow. The original poster had given birth to yet another generation—this time in orange—and the radius continued to expand. Sitting in the window at Lulu's, my local café, I could see the whole range of posters, hanging on the different street corners.

I marveled at Liz's executive abilities. She was CEO material: ambitious, determined, organized, and thorough. She understood PR, too, and she knew what she wanted. She could teach Lost Cats 101.

While my main career is that of a therapist, I found it useful to learn the art of business consulting. Many of my clients were professionals, business owners, and freelancers—people who are creatively successful, but overworked without the upside of improved results or increased income. Intelligence is not enough to be successful. You need to develop management skills, and be clear on your short- and long-term goals. You need to distinguish between impulsivity and genuine intuition when making business decisions. Self-doubt can interfere at any time, whether you're closing a million dollar deal or searching for a missing cat.

After a month of admiring Liz's take-charge behavior, I decided to call her. The posters were still up, but there was a chance that Sydney was napping at home with his supportive siblings. After three years of sleuthing, I'd concluded that the majority of owners tend not to remove their lost-cat posters, even after they've found their cat.

We agreed to meet at a French bakery for coffee at 9 a.m. Unfortunately, I arrived late—9:05, to be exact. I looked around. The café only had three tables. One was empty; two were occupied by couples. At 9:30, I went home and called her.

"You weren't there," she said. The CEO was grumpy. She'd waited for me until 9:03 and then left.

Didn't I deserve a five-minute grace period? I'd been tracking this story for a month! My two wayward minutes would go to the grave with me.

"I'm very sorry," I said. "Can we try again?"

"I'm not in the mood," she said. "It's a long story."

"We don't have to meet in person," I offered, feeling unfairly punished.

"A lot went on," she muttered ambivalently.

"Is this a bad time?"

"Well, it's complicated. It's been weeks."

Zak jumped up on my desk and stepped on top of Sydney's poster. I looked at him as if to say, "She's being difficult." He purred like the sound of a light rain hitting the roof. I spent another minute cajoling Anne into a better mood.

By the way, preparing people to talk about what was on their minds is part of the therapist's job description. Even though a client has chosen to go into therapy, he or she may still resent having to be there. One former client glanced at her watch every time after I opened my office door and greeted her in the waiting room. When I was late by a minute, she took offense. When I opened the door at exactly 3 p.m. sharp, she'd remark, "Great, we're starting on time."

During one session, after she'd ignored an empathetic comment from me, I sat quietly. I imagined that I felt like her boss and coworkers did—hurt and tired of being dismissed by her. She broke the silence. "Your tissue box has more tissues than the one on my side," I heard her say.

"Excuse me?"

"You gave yourself more tissues, and the client box is almost out of tissues."

"The clients use them more often," I said, without thinking. A moment later, I gathered my wits. "Do you really believe that I spend my time counting the tissues so that my clients can feel bad?" I decided my honest reaction could be therapeutic for her. She was looking for disappointments so that she could reject me before I failed her. What would she do with my confrontation?

"I was only kidding."

"No, you weren't," I replied. "Deal with your anger directly. What's it going to be?"

She'd never believe that I knew what it was like to be in that much pain, but I understood her secret belief system. Hiding your needs feels better than acknowledging your need for others. I'd come out the other side, but I valued being connected to others more than I valued being right.

"Okay," she said, folding her arms, "I hate coming here. It's demeaning."

"And?"

"It's like paying someone to care. You're like an emotional prostitute."

"Thank you for reducing my life's work to streetwalking." I put my hands up in the air.

"I didn't mean it that way." Her eyes fluttered for a second.

"Yes, you did. If I'm using you, what are you using me for?"

She looked out the window. "To listen, I guess."

"You've made it clear that I'm a lousy listener. Why do you keep coming back? So that I can fail you some more?" I smiled a sliver wide.

"You know some of my history," she said, slowly, struggling to find her own conclusion. But now she was engaged in the real issue.

"Is that enough?"

She looked at me like a feral cat surveying a human.

"Would you like to be known?"

She gave two tiny nods of her head. Yes.

When cat owners and clients are reluctant to speak—whatever the reason—I respect their limits at face value. Often, though, you can tell they haven't quite made up their minds so I encouraged Anne to talk about Sydney. Once she warmed up, she told one red-hot story.

Anne's troubles began when she reached the bottom of the basement stairs. A slice of January cold slapped her in the face. "Honestly, I wasn't worried about Sydney," she said. "I just didn't expect it to be freezing."

In a three-story house, with four cats drifting from room to room, several hours might go by without one or the other making an appearance. As the day shuffled forward, she occasionally wondered why Sydney was being more elusive than usual. It probably meant that she was sleeping in an undisclosed location. "I'm not the hovering type," Anne said. "I like my cats to free range."

She was nominally concerned about Sydney, but she was upset about the temperature in the house. Why was it getting even colder? Maybe a window had cracked? Anne went down the basement stairs and zigzagged past the furniture and antiques until she discovered the answer. The open back door was graciously welcoming the wind. For a moment, she was confused.

Then clarity struck. The gasman hadn't closed the door tightly enough after reading the meter, and Sydney must have dashed out. "Not only did I have to pay an outrageous heating bill," she said, "but the gas company lost my cat."

Anne gathered the standard-issue cat-rescue equipment. "After work, I carried my flashlight and my cat's food bowl," she said. Then she added, "I basically trespassed all over other people's yards."

Her lost-cat posters had been successful. Sort of. Several people called. They'd seen Sydney prowling on two streets in particular. Anne gave a sick chuckle. Unfortunately, it was a rough area. "I looked behind bushes, garbage cans, and garages," she said, speaking fast enough to be a junior auctioneer. "It was a dark street. I couldn't decide if I was brave or insane. My original goal of stumbling upon Sydney had changed. Now I just wanted to stay alive and not upset any of the local businessmen . . . you know, by interrupting a drug deal."

In the second week of the search (the purple publicity campaign), Anne received a special delivery. Two college students rang her doorbell, and she opened the door to find one of them holding a squirming calico cat.

"Here's Sydney," he told her with pride.

"The cat wouldn't stop snarling and hissing," she said. "He was behaving more like a prisoner of war than a missing loved one." Finally kicking free, the Sydney look-alike sprung off the porch and ran home. "Kidnapping is a federal offense," she told them, trying not to laugh.

Several days later, during the orange-poster offensive, another student who lived nearby called Anne and announced, "I have your cat at my house." Anne's intuition told her it was another false alarm, but the young woman insisted. She couldn't risk not following up on the lead, so she left her office in the middle of the afternoon.

The young woman enthusiastically led Anne to the feline

detainee's quarters. Anne stooped down to get a closer look. "These angry yellow eyes glared back at me," she said. "They were shouting, 'Call my lawyer! I'm getting a restraining order!' It was the same calico the guys had captured the week before."

Three weeks later, nothing was funny. Too much time had passed, and Anne was feeling depressed. She sat at the kitchen table drinking tea, and an unfamiliar feeling of inertia overtook her. She tried to shake it. Crisscrossing the mental lines that divided the realist from the dreamer became more difficult. Her imagination wasn't going to soar, not today. Her mood blackened, and she wondered, "How long can I hold out?" She looked at the cold tea sitting in her cup and surrendered. Sydney was gone.

Sometimes I encourage clients to raise their voices in therapy. I encourage the quiet ones to deepen their tone or even yell, anything instead of swallowing the words that sit suppressed inside their throats. (The natural yellers I contain because they yell to avoid feeling.) I was imagining the words that skulked about inside Anne's head. It was a universal scream of helplessness. *It's not what I wanted. It's not fair. I miss you.*

But Anne wasn't the type to get all gushy. She was occupied with telling the story, which allowed her to avoid her feelings as she relayed the events surrounding them. She transfers her anxiety into organizing and articulating details. I'm used to that style. It has value. It allows a person to keep themselves ordered and in control while conveying essential information.

Anne may have thrown her fate to the gods, but fate had something to give back. "Then, and you're not going to believe this," she burst out, "a split second later, I had a mind-blowing experience." The kitchen wall spoke to Anne. "I heard one little meow." She jumped out of her chair and rushed to the wall, "Sydney?" She yelled the cat's name over and over, but the wall remained silent. It was exactly like talking to a wall.

"*Now* what do I do?" Anne said. "How do you rescue a cat trapped in a wall?" She mulled it over for a while, and then called the fire department. "After all," she reasoned, "they rescue people who are trapped behind burning walls." I was impressed with Anne's crisis-resolution skills. I was beginning to think that if for some reason I got stuck in a foxhole, and I could see the whites of my enemies' eyes, I'd want Anne to be my foxhole buddy. She'd get both of us out alive.

"But it's not like TV," Anne said. "I told them I grew up with *Leave It to Beaver* and TV firemen who did neighborly things, like rescuing cats stuck in a tree. The New Haven Fire Department said they wouldn't come over and look for Sydney. They said she's just a cat, not a person. I said, 'You need to rethink that position.'"

Undaunted, Anne continued to badger them. "Maybe the *Leave It to Beaver* analogy lacked gravitas," she told me. Finally, several firefighters drove over and examined her kitchen wall. They even brought in a machine that scans for shapes *inside* of walls, but nothing they found resembled the outline of a cat. Her disappointment was sidelined by the deafening sound of fire sirens honking in tandem. They continued—mercilessly—until two fire trucks stopped and blocked the street in front of her house. Eight firemen in full gear, including axes, hustled up the porch stairs and stampeded in different directions throughout the house. From the third floor, a fireman yelled down, "We hear meows in the attic!"

"Good work," Anne yelled back. "My other three cats have run up there, terrified!"

She liked the theatrics of the rescue, though. Having no fire to fight, the guys at the station house had decided to play a practical joke. They gave her Beaver on steroids.

When game time was over and the firemen had to go, Anne begged, "Please, could you do just one more thing." There was a small hole a couple of inches deep in the kitchen floor, which opened into the rafters of the basement ceiling. She persuaded the firemen to make the hole a little bit bigger, just in case Sydney had crawled through, but couldn't make the return trip. It was a longshot, she realized.

I was surprised to hear about a hole in the floor so late into the conversation. It seemed a huge detail to skip over. Anne explained that after finding the back door open during the storm, she'd also covered her bases indoors. In fact, the first place she'd checked was the hole, sticking her hand down into the basement and wiggling it back and forth while calling for Sydney. But her animal family wasn't sniffing around the hole, so she was sure that Sydney had slipped out the door—*carpe diem!*—even though it had been snowing furiously.

The firemen cut the hole and left. The house was quiet again, and Anne sat at the kitchen table drinking a fresh cup of tea, wondering if she was out of options. "And then I had a second mind-blowing moment," she said. Like a jack-in-the-box, Sydney's head popped up out of the hole, and then, in an instant, vanished.

Anne hunkered down on the floor and prepared for a long wait. She sat next to the hole and stared at it. She opened up a can of tuna and dropped it in. An hour later the jack-in-the-box sprang up again, but this time Anne was poised. She lurched forward, grabbed Sydney, and pulled her out.

Thin had become bone skinny—Sydney had lost five pounds. Anne had a hundred questions, but they were all variations on a theme. "What the hell happened?" Had she simply been exploring the hole? Or had Sydney gotten spooked and gone into the hole for hiding? Did she get stuck in part of the basement interior? Had she traveled to a different part of the house? Did losing five pounds allow her to wiggle free? Why didn't she make any noise for three whole weeks? And when she finally did speak up, why only one tiny meow?

There's another storied feline on the West Coast who'd pulled a similar three-week disappearing act. In 1998 Joni Mitchell channeled her lost-cat blues into the song, "Man from Mars." Joni's poetic lyrics captured Anne's particular experience. Joni imagined her cat roaming somewhere in the walls and the wiring in her house. The day after she completed it, her Abyssinian mix, Nietzsche, came home.

"Futile!" Anne declared. "Asking questions is futile." But she did have one for me. She mentioned that she might have come on a little too strong with the fire department. Perhaps she'd been too demanding. What did I think?

Anne typically answered her own questions. Her response to Sydney's don't-ask-don't-tell policy was an exception. My involvement, I assumed, would be primarily rhetorical. The strong-willed, like Anne, have already made up their minds by the time they've thrown out a question for others to chew on. It was more like I'd been given a minor role in a play—something with only two lines. I was grateful for the relative anonymity of the telephone while I reflexively nodded my head. "No," I reassured her. "You were worried about Sydney. Hey, a goat fights for her kid."

Her next question? She'd already answered that one, too. "What could I do to show my appreciation?" She wanted to thank the firemen for their help. "At first, I thought about offering them money, but that seemed gauche. But what do you get for a group of men? Also, what do you get that they could actually keep at the firehouse?"

Beats me.

"Then I thought about a bottle of wine," she continued, "but maybe that was illegal, since they were on the job, and instead of thanking them, I'd get them fired instead. So I ruled out a couple of six packs, too. A thank-you card seemed skimpy." Finally, her ethnic heritage came to the rescue. "Being Italian," she said, "I figured it out." She walked over to the firehouse and handed out boxes of New Haven's finest cannoli.

Kool Kat Jellybean

zany, playful, affectionate

spayed
shots

donation

KOOL KAT JELLYBEAN

Proust had the pleasure of biting into a pastry before his memory went spiraling back into the world of his youth. My journey began after I pilfered Kool Kat Jellybean's poster from VIDEO-CITY. Unfortunately, the only thing I was biting into was my lip. It turned out that Kool Kat was not a lost cat, and that what I had seen was, in fact, a *found* poster. But that's not what sent me in search of lost time. There was something about Kool Kat's owner, something about the full-bodied soprano voice, with its odd and memorable cadences. When I finished introducing myself there was a pause at the other end of the phone, followed by a gasp and a giggle. "You might not remember me," she said, accenting the last syllable of every word, "but I was a therapy client of yours a long time ago. It's me, Evelyn Jones."

I gulped.

There's a reason I don't announce that "I'm a therapist" while sleuthing. Therapists make people nervous. But this time I was the flustered party. I normally enjoy hearing from former clients; Evelyn was a rare exception.

She'd fired me.

It was the late 1980s when Evelyn entered psychotherapy.

She and her partner of five years were trapped in a break-up/ make-up cycle. Easily intimidated, Evelyn had buried her anger instead of expressing it.

At the time, I was a psychotherapist-in-training, a doctoral student receiving supervision. I longed for the days when I would feel wise, when I could feel confident that my clinical feedback was helpful for my clients. But I was inexperienced, and hadn't yet learned how to fill in the blanks after listening to only one side of a relationship. During one of Evelyn's separations from her partner, she made a heated decision to end the relationship—and I made the mistake of agreeing with her. I'd overidentified with my client's struggle not to feel devalued. "It made sense to break up," I told her, having lost sight of the fact that her desires would change, that leaving would eventually be replaced by longing.

Sure enough, Evelyn and her partner reunited. At our next appointment, I tried to put myself back in a neutral position, but it was too late. In Evelyn's eyes, I'd become a judge she had to defend herself against. Not yet having learned how to confront the people she was closest to, Evelyn fell back on what she *did* know. She broke up with me. She cancelled her appointments and wouldn't return my calls. I wanted to tell her that I was sorry.

One summer, several years later, I saw her downtown, smiling and holding hands with the same girlfriend. She still had her signature look—long, blonde hair, braided on one side. She looked happy. From afar, it seemed that time had served her well, even if I had not.

Treating one member of a couple is like conducting therapy while a ghost flutters about in the room. A client can't help but anticipate his or her partner's likely reaction to a hot-button issue. But more than simply haunting the session, the ghost partner acts as a second conscience on the client in the office. Even an otherwise put-together person will fear (and intensify) the anticipated consequences of disappointing a loved one. ("She'll sulk and I can't stand a night of that." "If I tell him things he doesn't want to hear he'll get mad at me.") The most crippling of fears is often left unspoken, "If my partner leaves me, it's my fault. I will have caused my own abandonment."

During our therapy sessions, Evelyn tried to find a path that felt right to her. ("Maybe I should live alone." "My partner gets angry, not me." "Maybe I should be with someone else.") But by never delving into any one path too deeply—by changing her mind frequently—she spared herself the fallout that comes with personal clarity.

Unfortunately, salvaging her self-esteem created a potentially fatal solution. By mischaracterizing her partner as the angry one, and herself as someone who "never gets angry," Evelyn shrouded her fear of abandonment. Instead, she engaged in an artificial set of questions that were seemingly worthy of endless pondering: "Should I stay or go?" When Evelyn made her temporarily triumphant decision to leave her partner, I sided with her as if one bold, singular move would solidify her independence. I was young, too. It was a milestone mistake for me and I sought further training because of it. Breaking up was too big of a leap for Evelyn, and not the central issue. She only wanted to say, "Listen to me and don't leave!"

Twenty years later, I had an opportunity to see how Evelyn had matured. She was amused by my investigations and genuinely interested in what I'd learned from other lost-and-found cat owners. We didn't speak about the past. She graciously agreed to tell me her story, and then added a caveat—I had to promise that I would never reveal her identity. "It's crucial that my rescue work stay anonymous," she muttered into the receiver. I was reminded of how self-conscious she could be. My curiosity was piqued, but I let it go—it was clear that Evelyn still needed a safe and confidential relationship. I readily pledged to protect it, and

I have. I've changed all descriptive information about her, but have left the heart of her story.

"My life's work," Evelyn said, referring to rescuing stray cats, "started by accident, on the job." I remembered that she'd had the distinction of being the first woman hired as a technician by a cable company.

Her first rescue cat was a real talker. He was persistent, too, letting out a long series of elongated meows into the hallway where Evelyn was on the job. With a cable box to install, she knocked on her customer's front door. The crooner cat lived in the apartment across the hall. "Maybe he was Siamese," she thought. "They like volume." She installed the box and left. Two days later, with another work order in hand, she parked her truck in front of the same building, took the elevator to the same floor, and heard the same cat cry out. This time his meows were rapid, constant, and high pitched. Evelyn asked her new customer about the cat.

"The apartment's empty," he said, impassively. Evelyn's hippie heart missed a beat. "They skipped out on the rent a few days ago. It was a family. There were five of them. They left the cat behind and locked the door."

Evelyn took a step back from him. He was part of the heartlessness—a white squall of words and rationalizations. She headed for the elevator. She could hear her heart beating for an entire floor of people who were missing their own hearts. The customer stepped into the hallway and shouted, "What about my cable?"

Evelyn found the superintendent. He didn't want to get involved. "I'm putting my job on the line," she told him, figuring out he needed to hear that she would assume all of the responsibility. They went to the apartment and he unlocked the door. Waiting on the other side was a skinny brown tabby that Evelyn swept up into her arms and scratched his neck. "You're going home," she told him as his dark eyes scanned her face. "It was the beginning of my life's calling."

"I see the stuff of urban legends," Evelyn said, referring to her current life of searching for feral cats in the city. "This has taken me into places I would never have known about—stray cat colonies with populations in the double digits. They live in abandoned buildings, in between crumbling fallen bricks and the holes in the foundations. They can live anywhere, like furry cockroaches." In the United States, the Feral Cat Coalition believes that there are over 60 million strays living wild. The U.S. Department of Agriculture figures are equally grim for the cats that once had owners—over 5 million cats are abandoned each year.

Evelyn wears her search-and-rescue uniform during the summer months: long, thick pants; sturdy boots; full sleeves; and rubber gloves. She tries to determine whether or not each stray can be domesticated. Older feral cats are impossible to change, but kittens up to about ten weeks old still have a chance to attach to humans. She also looks for cats that have been forced onto the street; she'll take a chance on them if they seem nonaggressive. She uses Havahart traps designed to catch a live cat. (*Tip:* They can also be used for a skunk; one- and two-door models available.)

Over 100,000 feral cats are estimated to be living in New York City. It's not just feral cats that contribute to the growth of the feral population. Many unneutered domestic cats abandoned under one year of age are having multiple kittens. An unspayed female is capable of having a litter every four months.

For two decades, and without organizational assistance, Evelyn has paid for neutering, vaccination, and food, while continuing to place hundreds of adopted cats in loving homes. She limits the number of foster cats residing with her to two at a time, but still describes her supermarket shopping as mostly cat food. "I gave up trying to explain," she said. "It looked like I had two hundred cats." She laughed at herself. "You can call me a Cat Lady if you want," she said putting a very positive spin on my obsessive cat owner category.

Like many women I'd spoken with, Evelyn had rehabbed the pejorative term, "Crazy Cat Lady." The phrase had reached its satirical high point at the Web boutique "Crazy Cat Ladies and the Gentlemen's Auxiliary," where you can actually purchase a Crazy Cat Lady in action-figure form. Her uniform is comprised of a "never-out-of-my-pajamas" look and a crumpled bathrobe, each pocket filled with a cat.

I thought Evelyn would appreciate hearing a story about one of her sister Cat Ladies, a cat rescuer who lives in Los Angeles.

"I have a guest room for cats," the LA Cat Lady had told me.

To which I had replied, "What about the amenities? Room service or catch your own?"

"That's funny," Evelyn said with a laugh. Then we shared a moment of silence. "You're sure my identity will stay confidential?" I reassured her again. Had I said something to undermine her trust in me?

Evelyn continued. Her accountant wanted her to itemize her charity expenses, or at the very least, affiliate with a nonprofit cat organization so that he could lower her taxes. "He's going to kill me if I don't keep better records," she said, sounding unmoved, "but I can't be bothered. This is my version of going to church."

The interview was flowing again, and then I heard, "This is confidential, right?" I was at a loss. It felt like I was trapped with Rain Man.

"It's confidential," I said wearily. "This interview wasn't meant to create anxiety. We don't have to continue."

I steered the conversation to a lighter, final note. "I'm glad you found your life's work, and thank you—." But she cut me off.

In a quavering voice she said, "I believe, uh, that giving, uh, shouldn't, um, bring attention to you. I just don't want people to know."

Evelyn is fierce about her life's calling. She may pray at the altar of feline devotion, but she screens would-be cat owners with the rigor and strictness of an old-style nun standing at the front of a classroom, ruler in hand. For the safety of the cat, she's learned to anticipate the future sins of the adoptive owners. It sounds cynical, but from a psychotherapist's point of view, it's spot on—current behavior suggests future behavior. With one swift consultation (not unlike a therapist), Evelyn determines her client's suitability. She shared her concerns with me.

"Sometimes it's their appearance," she said, referring to people who are unwilling or physically unable to take care of a cat, "and sometimes it's what they say. I can tell by their attitude toward medical care. If they don't have a vet, I offer them a referral. If they don't mention a friend or a relative who has one, you know they aren't going to get one."

Once she even cancelled an adoption when a father ignored his child's rough play with her kitten. "Are the parents teaching their kids how to play gently," she said, "or do they just yell at them?"

Adoption was more complicated than I'd realized. Take dog owners, for instance. Evelyn instructs them to bring their dogs over to the meeting. She lets the prospective owners believe that she's observing their dog's behavior, when, in fact, she's more focused on their capacity for handling two species that don't get along.

Many of us live in apartments where pets are forbidden and break the rules, anyway. Not, however, if Evelyn knows about it. One young couple adopted a kitten from her, and a week later, Evelyn made a standard follow-up call. Kitty was supposed to have remained a secret, but the secret meowed, and the couple had to give her away. After that she implemented a new policy. "Renters have to bring their leases," she said, "and show me where it says that pets are allowed."

She's also ever-vigilant about foiling the recruitment plans of research laboratories. In order to complete an adoption, Evelyn requires a monetary donation. She said, with a verbal punch, "Labs won't pay to experiment."

I'm glad I got over my initial humiliation and heard about Evelyn's midlife bloom; it also gave me a yardstick with which to measure my own growth. I'd always looked forward to being an older therapist, one implicitly perceived to be credible. Some of my early clients, understandably, had been dubious about my capacity to help. ("What do you know about grown kids, or death, or divorce?" they would challenge. "Or losing a business that you spent years building?") Evelyn's therapy would have proceeded differently if I'd known then what only age had been able to teach me—you can do a thousand things right as a therapist, but it's what you do wrong, and how you handle it, that matters most. As one client told me, "Therapists almost never say they're sorry."

Perhaps Evelyn will always battle her own extremes; she's like a superhero who manages dual identities. When she's fighting for truth, justice, and the feline way, Cat Lady leaps into a cityscape of fallen bricks and crumbling mortar. She rescues the forgotten ones, fights the selfish, and protects the innocent. But when she sets aside her Cat Lady persona, she also sets aside her personal rights. Mild-mannered Evelyn, self-effacing and fumbling, worried about telling a loved one (and even her therapist) the barest of her needs. I also needed to remember that her core was resilient. If motivated by injustice, she could summon her strength at will.

She seems happy. After twenty-five years, she and her life partner, an artist, are still together.

Kool Kat was happy, too. His life as a stray was over. The church of Evelyn had found him a home.

LOST
CAT

Silver tabby lost from the
Mush Mush Adventures downtown office
15 years old, neutered male; looks
just like "Danger" the dog yard cat. (Acts
like him too!) Very precious to me. Answers
to "Kitty". *Please* call (344) 555 7861

DANGER AND KITTY

My surprise reacquaintance with Evelyn became a turning point. The cat-poster trail was no longer the same. I was curious and more curious. How had so many cat stories lead back into an examination of my own life when, in fact, I'd begun studying cat posters to learn about the lives of other people? Eccles, Maddy, and Maomy haunted me. Niko, Wuss, and Sydney made me fall in love with my own neighborhood all over again. Tori was a lightning strike from the past. Apparently I was on an odyssey although I didn't know how to define the endpoint. I wasn't even sure what the goal was, only that I knew I should continue.

Instead of tiring of lost-cat posters, after more than three years, I was invigorated by the possibilities that they represented—new places and people and cats. For instance, Shelby's family had increased my understanding of living in New York. I was peeking into the lives of those who would have remained anonymous, the ones you glimpse through the window as you pass by their apartment or house. I was visiting their secret room, a room lit with cheer or grief and solitude or companionship. Almost all people are captivated by stories—regardless of the medium—television, books, movies, video games, and theater.

I have the wanderlust gene. It's my maternal inheritance. At seven years old, my brother Richie and I walked home from school and discovered our station wagon packed with luggage. During the day, my mother had decided that we should go to Florida for the Christmas break. When my father came home from his school, she informed him, too. We kids crammed into the backseat and started bickering about who got to sit next to the window. My dad drove south. My mother, looking through the front windshield, beamed with pleasure.

Now, when I visit a new city I imagine myself living there. If I love it, I have regrets upon leaving. If only I had nine lives. Although I was very busy with two. The sleuth discovered that a lost-cat poster place could become a calling card. What better way to connect to people and their real lives while offering them empathy, too? Certain lost-cat posters were irresistible. I'd always wanted to take a trip to Alaska, and when I did, I fell in love with Danger.

We were leaving Anchorage to drive through the Alaskan rainforest, and that day the summer forest was covered in sunlight. No matter how fast or far we drove on Route 1, I never seemed to get any closer to the edge of a huge blue sky. Blooms of purple and red wildflowers lay scattered across low-lying fields that stretched on into the horizon. Karis, Jeff, and Valerie loved the landscape, too.

Just outside of Seward, I stopped at an all-purpose gas station the size of a big box store. But before I had a chance to inspect the heavy machinery, guns, and party supplies, I saw Kitty's photograph, replete with dogsleds, huskies, and snow, taped to the front door. The poster added a new dimension to my collection. It was a two-for-one: a lost-cat poster and an iconic portrait of Alaska. It would be a vacation keepsake.

I'd been studying posters for about four years, and while

Karis and my brother Jeff walked the aisles of the convenience store, I handed the poster to Valerie, my lanky niece, now twelve years old. "Look," I said with a smile. Val read the poster out loud, but stopped when she bumped into the phrase, "looks just like 'Danger' the dog yard cat."

"That's weird," she said. "What's a 'dog yard cat'?"

"I have no idea." Kitty, apparently, resembled another local cat. Maybe this one was a celebrity?

"Why do you want a lost-cat poster?" Val asked. "It's so sad."

I explained the Nancy Drew perspective. "I even have her initials." Val gave me a blank stare. I switched to a different topic—curiosity. "Have you ever wondered who the owners are?" Val stayed quiet. I quickly moved on to the hope project. "I'm hoping to hear that the cats were found, but even if they weren't, maybe the owners were still able to find peace and happiness."

"You're weird," she said.

"Thanks."

She smiled, and I went back to musing on the missing cat.

I knew only one thing for sure: the owner was a woman. Her name wasn't on the poster, but men tend not to use the phrase, "Very precious to me." And even though, in the smaller photograph of Kitty, there appeared to be a large male hand wrapped around him, I stuck with my original profile. That could have been anyone holding on to Kitty.

There was good news, too. Judging by the date of the poster, Kitty had only been missing for two days. I presumed the owner would need time to find him, so I packed the poster in my luggage and we headed toward our cruise ship. Once we were onboard, we sailed into fjords and past islands thickly forested all the way down to the rocks at the water's edge. We witnessed the graceful airborne arc of baby dolphins. *These are memories in the making,* I thought. It will be difficult to leave Alaska.

Karis seemed to be napping whenever these magnificent creatures swam by. "You missed Flipper," we told her. She woke up to a second news report. "You missed Moby-Dick." The third time that Karis woke up from her nap, she said, "I know, I missed tea with the Loch Ness Monster."

But the more miles the ship traveled, the more I understood how microscopic we all are. The northeast seems claustrophobic in comparison to the length and breadth of a land uninterrupted by commerce. I wouldn't want to lose my cat in Alaska.

So how would someone find Kitty? Divide the population by the land mass, multiply that by the average distance any given cat might wander in a day, add variable X, and throw in my experience with rural cat owners, most of whom never found their missing pets. The math wasn't looking good. It's too few people in too large of an area to notice a stray. Carnivores are always lurking, and cats frequently wander away when it's time to die.

Imagine my surprise, then, when I spoke to Kitty's owner two weeks later from New York, and learned that he'd been found.

"Kitty was discovered six days later," a woman said, "sitting on the side of the road, near work." End of story. Maybe it was a regional style I hadn't encountered before: simple prose, no hyperbole. Even so, it seemed atypical. Where was the excitement? *I found Kitty!* Most owners wax effusive about recovering their cats, and they readily offer at least a few details. It's a two-story minimum. Where was the heartache and drama? I tried a few more questions. Was it a busy street? Did Kitty seem scared? She offered a few more clichés. "Yes, it was lucky. He's a sweet cat."

I was turning this oddity over in my mind when the woman threw me a curveball. She said, in a warm but no-nonsense tone, "Let me give you the owner's cell phone number. She's very interesting. You should call her."

"I thought you were the owner," I said. During previous conversations, whenever I spoke with someone who wasn't the cat's owner, they'd immediately clarified the relationship.

"No, I just work for her," she said.

I hung up and eagerly dialed the other number. The owner, Madeleine, answered her cell phone, but our conversation buckled as she shouted to someone nearby who apparently couldn't hear her. Finally, she put me on hold. The phone crackled for several minutes. When she got back on the line, the crackling made for disjointed dialogue and overlapping conversations, but it didn't seem to faze her.

"Kitty disappeared because we'd just moved and he didn't know the area." The "we" referred to herself and Kitty, although until recently, "we" had included a boyfriend. "My ex doesn't think his moods are a problem," she said, still bewildered by her boyfriend's inability to grasp the obvious reasons for their breakup. "I'm tired and I'm mad," she said, without conviction. Madeleine seemed to be grappling with post-breakup blues and frenetic misfires. One minute you're feeling energized, the next minute you're lost.

She and her boyfriend had split up and reunited many times. I listened casually, but I didn't think their relationship was over. In my experience, couples break up for good when there's indifference, not when there's passion (even if it's angry passion). And these ties were deep. They co-owned the dog sled company. Madeleine was proud to be a musher.

"I built the business, and now he has it," she said, "That's not right." It probably wasn't, but I was more intrigued by her cat's reappearance. "And my mother wants me to find a new business," she said. Madeleine was working part-time at a bus company and none too happily. "But I want to go back to mushing."

My natural response was, "Why does your mother want you to change careers?"

Characteristically, she answered a different question than the one that I had posed. "I love being outdoors," Madeleine said, before pausing and adding: "The boyfriend thing is too up and down. My mother just wants the best for me. I built the business. I'm a hard worker. I don't mind it."

I'm used to people taking a long time to get to their point, but it finally occurred to me that I needed to put on my shrinking cap. If I'd been thinking clearly I would have realized—this rambling oral memoir had started after I had asked my initial question: "How did you lose your cat?"

"So what happened to Kitty?" I asked again, trying to steer the musher back onto her trail.

"He didn't know the area," she said. Then I heard an echo of my brief interview with her employee: "Kitty was discovered six days later, sitting on the side of the road, near work."

Same words, same delivery. The news of Kitty's return was delivered like a statistic: the gross national product up by 2 percent, one cat found, and soybean prices stayed even. No big deal. Madeleine and her employee weren't falling into any of the categories on my cat owner personality graph. I'd originally pegged them for obsessives, because of the poster and the "very precious to me" line, but suddenly the Alaskan wilderness woman and rapid-fire speaker had lost her voice concerning the topic of her missing cat. She could only muster the words; "Kitty was discovered six days later, sitting on the side of the road, near work."

While I was contemplating an appropriately neutral response, Madeleine flipped the focus of the conversation onto me. Where was I from? Did I have a cat? Did I write for a newspaper? After I told her that I didn't know if or when I'd be published, her voice lightened and she seemed relieved. She fell silent. The cackling noise on the line disappeared. For the first time, it was quiet. I was in the eye of the storm. Madeleine, it seems, was gathering momentum. Five seconds later, with the energy of a runaway train, she blurted out, "Do you want the real story?"

If I smoked, I would have lit a cigarette.

In film noir, the femme fatale keeps the truth to herself, but the audience cuts her some slack because she's been hurt or betrayed or abandoned, and she's hostage to some guy she loves and hates. We feel for her. I raced from one thought to another. Crime? Cover-up? Conspiracy? Who was the femme fatale? Madeleine? Was it the employee? I ruled out Kitty, as he was a boy. "I thought you were telling me the real story," I said.

"I was sneaking into my office at four a.m." She lowered her voice. This would be the moment when the background music fades and a dangerous motif begins.

"When my partner and I split up, it was messy," she said. "There's bad blood right now." The plot was thickening. Ex-boyfriend/ex-business partner and, somehow, Kitty got caught in the middle. At four in the morning.

"I snuck in with a secret key," Madeleine said.

I wondered what she meant by a *secret* key. *Secret* as in a hide-a-key squirreled away near the office door? Or secret as in the boyfriend didn't know she had a second set of keys?

"Why doesn't your mother like him?"

"My mother told me to get out of the relationship," Madeline said, clearly unsure about the soundness of the advice. "She doesn't think John's good for me. He gets into arguments."

If Madeline felt she had to keep a secret key in case the relationship went south, I'm siding with Mom.

"Why did you sneak into your office to begin with?"

"I had to get important paperwork," she said. "I had to break into my office."

Kitty had been missing for six days at that point, but right as her "Watergate"-style burglary was in progress, he reappeared, walking in through the office's open door. The important paperwork remained a mystery. Because Madeleine was keeping her activities under the ex-partner's radar, she devised an official story: "I found him by the side of the road. *Psst,* pass it on."

Madeleine said that in time her off-the-record confession could go public and that was why she'd wanted to know if I was a writer. "In a year, you can tell the story," she said. "It's enough time for the bad blood to die down."

But I wasn't so sure about that. Some guy would come along, maybe the same one would come back. I imagined the couple's session. She and her boyfriend would arrive at my office. The skeptic, typically the reluctant partner—in this case, the moody boyfriend—is silently angry and deeply confused. He avoids eye contact with the therapist. "I don't need a stranger, particularly a know-it-all therapist, telling me how to lead my life!" The partner who actually believes in therapy, Madeleine in this case, appears weary, sad, stuck, but momentarily eager because a third, *neutral* party is present and may be able to offer help.

They both feel raw, like they've had to chew on their own muscle to keep the relationship alive. Moreover, each one believes that "despite my best efforts, the relationship is doomed." Why is the relationship imploding? In my experience, two intolerable fears exist simultaneously and unconsciously within each partner. The first fear silently screams, "I'm unlovable," so "it must be my fault." The second intolerable fear shouts: "My partner is the one who's incapable of loving." Either way, both fears lead to the same unwelcome conclusion—feelings of abandonment. Eventually, the relationship will end.

If you reduce a couple's fighting to its essence and remove the actual content of the fight, a relationship can be seen as two scared people grappling with fears of abandonment. Instability in a relationship is the result of both partners acting out their internal struggles on each other. Within the same fight, they alternate between blaming themselves and blaming the partner. If it's *your* fault, I can accuse, judge, blame, criticize, withdraw, get angry, and so on. If it's *my* fault, I'll allow myself to be judged and demeaned or become passive aggressive, take a martyr role, and so on.

One thing I'm sure of as a therapist is that long ago a series of emotional breaches occurred within the relationship of the fighting couple, shredding trust and emotional safety. Now, even the most casual of questions can stir dormant feelings of disappointment. "What's wrong?" The passive response avoids conflict: "Nothing, I'm tired." The aggressive response seeks conflict: "Nothing. What's wrong with you?"

I often hear, "Doctor, should we break up or not?" Honestly, I don't know. If partners have the desire to change themselves and learn empathy for each other, they probably will stay together. Sometimes filing for divorce is the big wake-up call. Affairs are always effective at getting your partner's attention, but the damage done may be the most lasting effect.

What was Madeleine doing for love? Her home, her job, and her relationship were in disarray. She kept a secret key, indicating that they'd fought many times before and she'd lost. She couldn't even access her business and both her mother and her employee wanted to protect her. Then she lost her precious cat.

From her side of the story, the boyfriend had "moods." Plural. "He got into arguments." A partner's changing moods, in my experience, tend to foreshadow a shift in the rules. The spouse is at the mercy of the latest decree. Fair and unfair become relative. Part of my job is to sit ringside while the "moody" one provokes a fight. For decades, I've watched both men and woman throw punches.

The couple exhibited all four of the chronic behaviors that are known to destroy marriages: criticism, contempt, defensiveness, and stonewalling. According to marriage expert and researcher John Gottman, Ph.D., the chronic presence of these behaviors signifies that the end is near. He refers to them as the "Four Horsemen of the Apocalypse."

Each "Horseman" paves the way for the next. Criticism refers to attacking your partner's character. Examples include "you always" or "you never." Of course, if one partner has ignored the legitimate requests of the other, it encourages the aggrieved to escalate. Contempt, considered the most destructive and abusive style of conflict, stems from resentment. Examples include insults, sarcasm, mocking, rolling one's eyes, and name-calling. Defensiveness means avoiding responsibility and playing the victim instead. "I wouldn't have a problem if you didn't . . ." Stonewalling means refusing to participate. Eventually, one of the partners refuses to participate in the relationship and ends it.

Whatever other patterns existed between Madeleine and her boyfriend, I suspected that the "secret key" signified not only her need for physical accessibility, but may have been emblematic of their emotional dynamic, as well. Listening to her brief story, it was apparent that she liked to converse, she needed people, and was welcoming of advice and support from others. Of course, if her boyfriend arbitrarily decided that "this conversation is over," her anxiety would shoot sky high. If she boisterously pursued him, adding a few accusations and criticisms, it would only reinforce his contempt. Initially, he may have emotionally stonewalled her, but over time it manifested as a literal wall. With a door. And a secret key.

What makes love last? After videotaping thousands of couples, Gottman learned that a couple needs a minimum daily ratio of five positive interactions to one negative interaction. That's a ratio only to *not* get divorced. Happy couples have even higher ratios, in the range of twenty to one. Positive interactions include offering eye contact, affection, verbal support, gift giving, etc.

If your intentions are to be kind, it doesn't take a lot of effort to behave in a kind manner. Smile. Once in a while squeeze your partner's hand. Don't roll your eyes when they say they want to find a new job. Clean up. Say, "You look nice." Happy couples have learned how to yield, receive, fight fairly, offer empathy, and understand their partner's particular strengths for resolving conflict. For instance, if one spouse likes to talk about problems and the other thinks before speaking, couples need to meet in the middle. The talkers learn to be more efficient in what they say and back off, but the quiet ones reward the talkers by offering specific times to eventually share their thoughts.

The science of happy couples also found that keeping your heart rate at ninety-five or lower allows a productive conversation to take place. Restless, outdoorsy Madeleine had the energy of a stallion. Her resting heart rate must have hovered at ninety-four. She had an infectious energy, too. Despite her current circumstances, she didn't complain about (or even badmouth) her ex-boyfriend. Instead, it seemed as if she was remembering who she was and where she'd been. She was tracking her own emotional life. Where had she gone off the trail?

More than anything else, I thought that Madeleine needed to listen to herself and make her own decisions. It sounded like she gave away her power to just about everyone. She was even telling me too much, giving me the whole story, even though it conflicted with her own plan to keep it all under the radar. I knew that Madeleine was intrepid. She was entrepreneurial and hardworking, but I wanted her to use a different courage. The courage to make her own emotional decisions—right or wrong. Madeleine needed time to develop, but discovering who we are can take a lifetime. Carl Jung, the father of depth psychology, believed that we didn't reach our emotional adulthood until our mid-fifties. (Personally, I find that encouraging.)

But I didn't want Madeleine to give up her spunk, not that she was in any immediate danger of losing her resilience to recover from a mishap. "The picture's fabulous," I said, referring to the poster. "Your cat's standing on a dog sled. It's what everyone imagines Alaska to look like."

"Oh, that's not a picture of Kitty," Madeleine said casually. I felt a jolt. "That's a picture of Danger, the dog yard cat at the kennels. I didn't have any pictures, but my Kitty looks exactly like Danger."

I'd been duped. Twice. Wasn't that the plot twist of every crime movie? So *she* was the femme fatale—I'd fallen for Kitty, who was, in fact, Danger. That made me the foil; like Jimmy Stewart after he races to the top of the stairs only to take the fall for a murder. At the end of the phone call, she'd offered one last confession. I had vertigo.

WHERE'S JOE?

HAVE YOU SEEN JOE?

He's been missing since Friday, July 5.

He's a 7-year old, black and white male
cat weighing about 13lb.

If you have seen him please call
(434) 555-8122

VANCOUVER JOE

We were supposed to be celebrating Karis's graduate degree, summa cum laude. But after we arrived, Nancy Drew discovered a killer cat-poster case. Karis became the reluctant chum. We had just flown over the white-capped Rocky Mountains across Canada and landed in Vancouver, a gem of a city bordered by the sea. The air was moist and the landscape a lush green. We took a taxi to our bed-and-breakfast while the clouds summoned all their shades of gray. While we stood on the sidewalk nervously double-checking our itinerary for our luxury B&B, the cab driver sped off, leaving us in front of a crooked house, a cement lawn, and a ceramic donkey. The plastic gnome with the big red nose was the deal breaker. I stepped into leadership mode.

"It's your fault," I said, smiling, to Karis. "You made the reservation." We headed downtown to find a real hotel, oblivious to the not-for-tourists neighborhood around us. We heard a variety of foreign languages. My cell phone was dead.

It began to pour, but we sloshed our way through a mile of Vancouver's homeless headquarters and numerous sidewalk drug sales. Guys followed us, asking, "Want some good pot?"

"No," Karis replied. "We prefer to die of natural causes."

We ran underneath a store's awning and that's when I saw the poster hanging in the window. The poster featured an endearing photograph of tuxedo Joe curled in the sink, along with the charming headline: WHERE'S JOE? I'm a sucker for a cat in a sink so I couldn't wait to get to a hotel and call the owners. But several miles later, after we finally reached downtown, we discovered that China, Paraguay, *and* Hungary were in town for an annual fireworks competition. "No hotel rooms anywhere?" I repeated, not calmly while our wet clothes dripped onto the marble floor. The desk clerk at the Radisson took pity on us and motioned us to take a seat in the lobby.

Karis sat glum-faced.

Then the concierge told us to follow her. We were led to our accommodations. But after moving a table, in the conference room, to make way for the rollout bed, I wrenched my neck. Karis dug through her luggage and gave me her last Advil. The ice pack took twenty minutes to arrive, but I dialed with my good arm. That's when I learned, "Cat home."

The grandfather of a three-generation Asian family living together in a single house answered the phone when I called. His accent was thick and his English minimal. He answered most of my questions with short phrases locked into staccato beats. "Window, garage, lock, people move, house empty, man find cat, call landlord, landlord come, cat free." He ended the story by repeating the words, "Joe found seven day, landlord come eight day. Cat home."

The presentation seemed chaotic, but the story was simple— Joe had been missing for seven days, then the neighbor discovered him in an unoccupied garage. Apparently, while the former tenants were busy packing, Joe had sniffed his way into the garage. When they finished, they locked the house, locked the garage, and drove away, completely unaware of Joe's presence.

A week later, a neighbor peeking through the window happened to see Joe trapped inside the garage. He told Joe's family, then Joe's family told the landlord, who showed up the following day to set Joe free. I tried to elicit a few more details about the rescue, but the grandfather replied with an excited, "Cat home, cat home!"

In spite of the conversation arrhythmia, this appeared to be a story about coordination: the neighbor, Joe's owner, and the landlord functioned like the cogs and wheels of a well-oiled clock. I bought the clock. I didn't suspect that it was telling the wrong time.

A few weeks later, after we'd returned to New York, I got caught in a thunderstorm and it reminded me of all the rain in Vancouver, and of Joe. Was he really all right? There was just something *about* that trip to Vancouver. Nothing was quite as it seemed. Had Joe really survived an entire week without food or water? I decided to call back.

This time, a young man (perhaps in his twenties) answered the phone. His voice was sharp and articulate, without any trace of an accent. "We couldn't figure out where Joe was," Lin said politely. He told me that everybody loved Joe, but that his seventeen-year-old sister was the cat's official owner. She made the poster.

Lin's sister had adopted Joe the kitten when she was ten years old. He had always traveled about, from the bathroom sink to the outdoors and everywhere in between. He was friendly and liked to be in the company of people. He was a snuggler, and not used to being alone.

Lin's story was similar to his grandfather's. Joe must have snuck into the garage while the tenants were moving. A neighbor finally saw him through the window and informed Lin's family. Joe's predicament fit the missing outdoor cat hypothesis. Assume that an outdoor cat is not hiding, but is sick, trapped, or dead.

"When Joe was finally free," Lin said, "we could see that he'd lost a lot of weight."

"Was he okay?"

"He's a fatty," Lin said playfully. "He's already putting the pounds back on. We spoil him." The owner profile came into sharp focus. "Spoiling," can only belong in the obsessive category.

But before I could ask about the rescue itself, Lin casually added, "Joe was discovered after five days, but the landlord didn't come until the eighth day."

I looked at my notes. Had I written down the wrong numbers? "Your grandfather said that Joe was found on the seventh day and then rescued the next day."

"No," Lin said firmly. "It took several days to reach the landlord, because no one seemed to know who he was. We had to find someone who had his phone number, and when we called him, he didn't call us right back. So we had to wait another day."

But Joe had been found, and, while days five, six, and seven rolled by, he'd remained un-rescued. I was stunned. Rescue missions in the past had offered only two possible outcomes— either the cat was saved, or lost for good. How could waiting even be considered a viable option?

"You mean no one tried to rescue Joe?" I said, still searching for an answer that mirrored my thinking.

"We waited," Lin said evenly.

I didn't know what to think. It's not that I expected others to behave as I did. On the heels of a sixty-second reading by a chain-smoking psychic I'd broken into my neighbor's house and rescued my cat. But the family's inaction seemed just as unusual. "Was waiting the only available option?" I asked.

"Oh, yes, many discussions took place, back and forth between the younger and older family members," Lin said. His words sounded so formal.

"What were the discussions about?"

"The younger people didn't want to wait, but the elder relatives thought it would be disrespectful."

"The young people wanted to break in?"

"Yes, but the elders wouldn't approve. They said that it was the landlord's property. He'd be mad."

"Your parents also agreed?"

"They agreed with my grandfather."

The youthful contingent kept a vigil outside the garage. The roof leaked. Noses flattened against the garage window, they watched Joe lick the water from a puddle of rain.

"Did waiting upset you?" I asked.

If Lin had been frustrated by the decision, or if he'd thought it should have been handled differently, he wasn't going to say so. At least not directly. Instead of answering my question, he spoke in generalities. "It was difficult for the family." He wouldn't reveal family discord to a stranger, and I understood that, but I was hoping to hear the particulars, to learn how each generation had negotiated for their beliefs.

Later on, I realized I'd had a knee-jerk reaction to the story about Joe's rescue. I was an American, responding from within my culture's value system: self-reliance, control, and individual choice. *Someone should have rescued Joe immediately, by any means necessary!* I had to pause. My feelings stemmed in part from my personality, but were also shaped by the culture I grew up in. If I was a product of my culture; Joe's family was a product of theirs.

Notions of right and wrong are typically learned in the home. I always keep that in mind while conducting therapy. Of course widely differing cultures, ethnicity, and religion, influence any families' values. I try to sideline my cultural point of view. It helps me to psychologically wander alongside my clients as they describe their lives. Their world is layered, filled with current and personal history, and whether they're aware of it or not, it includes their cultural heritage. Even if their family crest reads, "We're a mutt."

Therapists need to understand what makes therapy helpful

or toxic to different groups in society. Monica McGoldrick, who wrote *Ethnicity and Family Therapy*, a pioneering family therapist, wanted to know how ethnicity and culture affected families in therapy. How do national origin, religion, family roles, attitudes about authority, and gender influence decision-making? Her research zeroed in on which groups are more likely to seek therapy and which groups avoid it and why? Asians, for example, are typically disinterested in psychotherapy; they don't like to disclose their private feelings to a stranger. Jewish people embrace self-exploration (see any Woody Allen movie). In general, Irish Catholics mistake sentimentality for their true feelings, but because they are rule bound, they ultimately blame themselves for even *having* feelings. The Polish prefer behavioral changes to insight.

Immigrant Asian families, in general, don't believe in sharing their problems with outsiders. Therapy is considered shameful. ("Only crazy people see a psychologist.") The one in charge of the family's well-being is often the father, and searching outside the family for help is considered shameful. It signifies his loss of control.

But I've had many first-generation, Asian American clients, and their issues apply to most immigrant families. They're caught with their parents in a poignant, and not necessarily mutually resolvable, struggle between two worlds. For example, first-generation children typically long to have an emotionally accessible father, but in the old order, a father showed his love by being a good provider—affection and praise weren't part of his parental responsibilities. In my experience, although both parties continue to love each other, the father never quite receives the respect he's looking for, and the adult children continue to feel mischaracterized.

Lin said that Joe's captivity had been difficult for the entire family. Each generation's storyteller had emphasized what was emotionally significant to him (and even had the numbers to back it up). The grandfather, originally from Hong Kong, seemed genuinely happy that Joe had been found, but his story also sounded like an Asian adaptation of *Do the Right Thing*. An individual's behavior reflects on the entire family, including its ancestors. During the grandfather's adolescence, societal cooperation mattered. Now, as the elder of the family, it was the grandfather's responsibility to maintain the family's honor and the social order. His storytelling focused on property rights, social relations, and harmony. He expressed his love by helping the family to keep its honor.

But love can't stop change. The grandfather's world coexists with modern times; his grandchildren were assimilating. Lin's story framed his generation's conflict—divided loyalties. They may love and respect their parents and grandparents, but they have their own needs and desires in a society that values informality, individualism, and self-expression. ("Joe, we're busting in.") Assimilation for the children of immigrants is an ongoing process. It never relents. In fact, that was their job. They were going to school and coming of age in a Western society that they clearly wanted to belong to. The cat's name made it apparent. He's the All-American—or All-Canadian—Joe!

What else was the younger generation learning? What about love? What were they learning to associate with it? We can take an educated guess by comparing the difference between two possible outcomes.

Scene one: The younger generation stands outside the garage window and stares at Joe trapped inside.

Scene two: They unlock the garage and free Joe.

In which scene is love more likely to become associated with loyalty or disloyalty? Or feeling burdened by love or respect and compliance? Which scene creates a split in the young ones between their feelings about love and their principles about love? Which scene encourages independence and Western values?

The family-cat debacle must represent the tip of the iceberg. This three-generation family has decisions to make on a daily basis, all tinged with underlying issues of assimilation versus tradition. Decisions, negotiations, and compromise are probably the stuff of everyday life.

What did Joe's owners do for love? It depends upon who you talk to.

<u>REWARD</u>

LOST CAT. FAMILY HEARTBROKEN

Loving PET LOST MONDAY, NOV. 16.
WEST 90th STREET VICINITY.
SMALL BROWN STRIPED FEMALE.
WEARING LEOPARD BROWN COLLAR.
Phone # AND ADDRESS ON TAG.
  HER NAME "<u>LUCY</u>"

PL<u>EASE HELP US</u> IF YOU SEE HER!

Lucy (cat)	Lucy (cat)	Lucy (cat)	Lucy (cat)	Lucy (cat)	Lucy (cat)
2 1 2 5 5 5 8 9 8 9	2 1 2 5 5 5 8 9 8 9	2 1 2 5 5 5 8 9 8 9	2 1 2 5 5 5 8 9 8 9	2 1 2 5 5 5 8 9 8 9	2 1 2 5 5 5 8 9 8 9

BROADWAY LUCY

Lucy's owner didn't exactly greet me with open arms. His behavior was characterized by a lack of conversational participation, as opposed to the robust and engaging social skills exhibited by regular and obsessive cat owners. "Hello" went swimmingly, I thought. But after I offered my standard introduction, he didn't say anything. I looked down at the poster. Lucy was dainty and pretty; her shy eyes seemed to avoid a full-blown look at the world. She wore a tasteful and slender leopard collar. Lucy was an uptown girl. I could hear Billy Joel in the background.

But as the seconds crawled by, I got the sense that I was humming on my own. Lucy's owner had me rethinking my taxonomy of cat owners. Perhaps I'd need a third category. "Cat Owner with an Attitude" seemed like a good working title. But then he spoke. He uttered one word. In a stirring British accent, he said Lucy's name, drawing out both syllables until it sounded like a question filled with disdain. "Lucy?"

The poster had been taped to a lamppost on the Upper West Side off Broadway, which has six lanes filled with speeding cars, taxis, and buses. "The poster you made was so sweet," I said manipulatively. In my warmest voice possible, I added, "I was hoping that you'd found her." Silence. As I waited for his next word I had a flashback of a conversation I had with another reluctant cat owner, a fellow who hadn't wanted to answer my questions, either.

Granted, I had a skewed sample, but the sullen subtype seemed to be a club for men only. When I had called to inquire about a sandy-colored cat named Bart Simpson who had disappeared at a highway rest stop in North Carolina, it seemed as if the owner's responses were restricted—under penalty of law—to monosyllabic answers. But before he hung up, he showed one act of initiative.

"Why do you care?" he asked.

Later that year I'd had another encounter with a male cat owner. After a three-day vacation, I'd returned home to find a lost-cat poster hanging on the telephone pole at the end of my driveway. It was a black-and-white Xerox—apparently the cat had disappeared two days earlier. I called and a male answered, but I could barely hear him:

"The connection is bad," I yelled.

He yelled, too. "I'm at a rock concert!"

"Did you find your cat?"

"No. Not yet." *Garble. Screech.*

"Who's looking for your cat?" I shouted into the phone.

"I had these tickets . . ." Pounding in the background.

"What?"

"I had these tickets and maybe he'll come home on his own."

"You'd be lucky," I screamed into the reverb.

It's a well-known fact among therapists that men, in general, are reluctant to talk, even after their wives and girlfriends drag them to couples counseling. A man will typically say, "I'm here because my wife wanted me to come." If I dig a little deeper, I usually discover someone who—for a variety of reasons—feels drowned out, or has given up on listening to his wife. In turn, she's escalated every minor interaction into a report card on the state of their marriage.

Occasionally, I see couples with my colleague, Dr. Peter Rothenberg. Men take advice from him that would backfire if it came from a woman. For example, during one couple's session, the wife offered to caulk their windows at home to save on winter-heating costs. "You ain't paying the utilities," her husband said. "What the hell do you care?" Peter addressed his brusque manner and suggested a few alternative responses, then added with a wink, "At night, if you want your wife to sleep with you, during the day, speak nicely to her."

Still, I find males to be easy clients. They don't want to process feelings like women do. They want information. But once they're engaged in self-exploration they quickly find the links between their past and current life problems.

Dean was a successful real estate developer with legions of friends. He married at age forty but divorced after four years and two kids. Dean's history was curious. He'd never been in love, but he competed for the most attractive woman in the room. As a teenager, he was short and studded with acne. His adult behavior toward women (pursue, catch, and release) he told me, was caused by childhood resentment. He didn't like to talk about his feelings.

Some months later, his emotional façade disappeared. "I used to tell people that I got into real estate because my father said it was a good business," he said "I made it up and half-conned myself into believing it. My father and I never had a single meaningful conversation. When I'm with my own kids," he continued, his eyes welling up with tears, "I worry I'm not a good father." His sexual conquests took on a new light. "I don't know what to do when I'm close to a woman, so I try to have sex. It feels better than not knowing who I am."

I find it gratifying when people become less guarded, but Lucy's owner wasn't ready to drop the façade just yet. His cat seemed headed for the cold case file. Then I heard a faint "Mmm."

Good, he still had a pulse.

"Look," I wanted to say, "I'm just a harmless lost-cat poster sleuth. If you do a background check, you'll see that I have a day job. People like to talk to me. They even pay me for it. Sometimes they even come early."

I considered offering him easier conditions for participation. Was Lucy alive? Tap once for yes, twice for no. But he lingered on the phone like he was waiting for a list of demands. ("If you want to see your precious Lucy again, send a hundred bucks in unmarked bills.")

That's when it hit me. He thinks I'm a con artist!

He had a point. A huge point. Con artists read lost-cat posters, too. And nowadays, any contact information listed on a poster could provide access to your personal life. Lost-animal Web sites warn pet owners against getting scammed. Don't include your name or address on the poster, and if you're offering a reward, don't name the amount. When writing an ad for your local paper or a Web site offer minimal information. Never list all of the cat's identifying marks. When a stranger calls, don't give them information that can be used to con you. For instance do not say: "Does the cat have a black smudge on his left paw?" Instead say: "Please describe the cat."

If you are advertising for a cat that you *found* and strangers call and claim that the cat as their own, let them describe their missing cat to you. Also make it clear to them that you will bring the animal to their home. Never go alone. Keep the cat in the car until you receive some proof of ownership-veterinary records and/or family photographs.

Scams come in different styles. One common scam involves teamwork. One of the thieves calls the owner of the missing cat and describes to them a *found* cat. After a few inaccurate details, the owner will realize that it's not a match. Meanwhile, the thief has learned important information about the missing cat from the owner, and the near miss has made the owner more vulnerable to the next caller who says, "I found your cat." Soon thereafter, the thief's cohort will call, offering a perfect match. Then, before the cat's been returned, the grateful owner is maneuvered into sending the reward money. Usually they need money to "ship" the cat back to the owners.

How do smart people end up being scammed? Vulnerability makes for cloudy thinking.

The long-distance scam is popular. Someone has read your lost-cat flyer or Web site ad. Unfortunately he's a "truck driver" who discovered your lost cat in his vehicle, but he's hundreds of miles down the road, and, he took your sick cat to the vet. If you would only wire him the reimbursement money, he'll be able to send your cat back home with a trucker friend who is heading toward your town.

A more vicious scam involves threats. The scammers saw your ad and pretend to have your missing cat, but they threaten to harm Fluffy unless you pay the ransom.

Adoptions, within the United States or from abroad, offer many scamming opportunities, too. An ad might say, LOOKING FOR A LOVING HOME, CAN'T AFFORD, or AM MOVING MUST GIVE AWAY. Although the adoption is free, you soon discover that there are shipping expenses. Even if you agree and pay the expenses, you may receive another message. The cat needs veterinary treatment or customs won't release the cat.

Evelyn Jones designed strict adoption policies in order to thwart scammers. She wanted to prevent adopted cats from being sold to research facilities. However, some thieves will simply steal pets from a yard or a parked car. Then they sell groups of them to other shady dealers, who, after forging paperwork, resell the cats to research facilities.

A special or unique breed is often at risk for theft because they fetch the most money on resale to an unsuspecting cat lover. I saw a cat poster of an ocelot in a store window in North Hollywood. Ocicats look like a cross between a tiger and a leopard. The heartbroken owners wrote that they were worried that their cat was among the permanently stolen.

Once I realized that Nancy Drew was under permanent suspicion I revised my attitude and removed Lucy's owner from the curmudgeon category. Exercising caution was important. And it was acutely disturbing to realize that the very charm of lost-cat posters—their honesty and vulnerability—were also the tools used to swindle an owner.

Con artists are everywhere. In fact, one estimate is that between 2 to 5 percent of the population is comprised of people who have no moral bearing—other than getting what they want. That means there are millions of people in every level of society that are amoral. They even come to therapy.

The voice is a pure instrument for detecting the truth. In fact, studies show that subjects can more accurately detect lying when they hear only the voice. But when the subjects heard the voice and saw the speaker's face at the same time they were less able to detect who was lying and who was telling the truth. Eye contact, facial expressions, and smiling can distract us from purely listening.

Decades ago, I realized that listening to new clients on my answering machine offered me a window into their state of mind. I could hear cadence, rhythm, energy, enunciation, clarity or confusion of message, confidence or heartlessness, sincerity or duplicity, and the intent to lie. Once, a woman who spoke in a hypnotic voice, like Lauren Bacall if she spoke with a Noo Yawker accent, introduced herself to me over the phone.

"Why do you want to come to therapy?"

"My fiancé has trust issues."

"Who doesn't he trust?" I asked, realizing that I instinctively didn't trust her.

"I'm an exotic dancer," she said, with the glory of an artiste who had abandoned pediatric surgery because the theater spoke to her soul. "My fiancé found out exactly what it is I do at work."

"What do you do that he didn't know about?" I was having very little trouble imagining her professional responsibilities.

"He didn't know that I do lap dances."

"Why didn't he know?"

"I lied to protect him. He wouldn't understand. Wouldn't you try to protect someone from getting hurt?"

"So what kind of therapy do you want? Individual or couples?"

"Yes, my fiancé doesn't trust me and he doesn't understand me."

Maybe I sounded as insincere to Lucy's owner as the exotic dancer had sounded to me. Since he was still on the line—and I wasn't asking any of the typical scam questions about the missing cat or the owner's family—I tried once more to convey my sincerity. Burning through my entire stockpile of personal warmth, I said, "I hope she's not wandering on the street." A few seconds later, he strung a sentence together.

In a tone I've used to inform telemarketers that I'm not interested, he said, "After five days, we heard a meow in the backyard of our brownstone." *Click.*

WE HAVE LOST MUFFIN

Muffin is a gray striped, very lovable
male cat.

He likes to sun himself on the sidewalk
on Leed Street and meet passersby

Muffin has a very distinctive meow.

Muffin has been missing since Monday,
September 14th.

If you have any information about him,
please call us at (881) 555-2311

OLD CAT
AND MUFFIN

The Japanese poet, Issa, wrote in the fifteenth century:

> Goes out,
> comes back,
> the loves of a cat.

The lost-cat poster read like the beginning of a sad haiku: WE HAVE LOST MUFFIN. It was taped next to the exclusive Wall-of-Shame bulletin board in Romeo's Market and Deli. Romeo was a big-hearted Italian who allowed his customers to pay by personal check. Those that bounced were hanging on a bulletin board of shame marked in red ink: "Insufficient funds."

The deli was one of those neighborhood fixtures where everyone seemed to gather. During the lunch-hour rush, customers would vie for shaded tables and chairs underneath the big yellow umbrellas, but there was one patron who preferred to face the sun. Muffin's big brother, Old Cat, a big gray tabby, who lunched at Romeo's as part of his daily ritual.

Old Cat lived in my neighborhood of New Haven, Connecticut, on a street graced by tall Victorian houses originally built for large families, but now populated by Yale graduate students.

Life is sweet for a cat living in a Victorian, napping the day away on a big front porch, watching the academics stroll by—Old Cat especially. Old Cat liked strangers. He liked what they could do for him. A food gigolo who never lunched alone, Old Cat would choose a different passerby to trail to the deli each day. Truth be told, I'd been known to throw some of Romeo's tuna under my chair for the big tabby. He didn't push or rub up against your leg or meow in that annoying "if-you-don't-feed-me-I'll-starve" act. He looked up at your eyes and waited. You began to feel compassion. ("Oh, I'm the one who forgot to feed him.")

Of course, he wasn't always Old Cat. He got his name during his adoption ceremony. He was way past his midlife crisis, the fling with his secretary, and the red sports car. Old Cat's morning routine could have been copied from the activities board in a Miami retirement home. The early hours were occupied with stretching on the sidewalk and bird watching. The stroll started just after noon, as he picked his passerby and followed him toward the ultra early-bird special—Romeo's lunch service.

Customers sitting at the outdoor tables fed Old Cat meatballs and chicken slices and tuna. Although Romeo rarely took a break from unloading and unpacking crates, sometimes he fed Old Cat, too, and when the feline was full, he'd ramble back home and take a long afternoon nap, waking up just in time for the three o'clock shuffleboard tournament.

Then Muffin arrived. He was a wisp of a silver kitten that chased shadows on the wall and pounced on his furry brother. He adored Old Cat. Sometimes they licked and cleaned each other, and sleeping together was *de rigueur*. When the students in the old Victorian wanted to find Muffin, they looked for Old Cat. On their daily stroll down to Romeo's, Muffin positioned himself in the rear flank, tagging along ten to twenty paces behind his best friend. For two years, through New England's frigid winters and sweat-soaked summers, the cats paraded over to the deli, and were never turned away hungry. Muffin and Old

Cat were as much a part of the landscape as the ear-splitting brakes of the Yale shuttle bus. The cats seemed to be safe.

Then, one summer, an unleashed dog attacked Old Cat and killed him. Everyone who knew Old Cat was devastated. The three students who'd been taking care of him were worried about Muffin—would he be all right without his friend and mentor? They kept him inside for a few days, but he wasn't used to staying indoors. When the students brought him into one of their bedrooms to play, he meowed in frustration. Other times, Muffin warbled mournfully. He missed Old Cat. The students decided to let him go outside.

Even though he was traveling solo now, Muffin kept to the old routine. He continued sunning himself on the sidewalk, following strangers to Romeo's, eating lunch, and then rambling home. After a few months, it was almost as if things were back to normal. The leaves were turning, their edges smudged with bits of gold and red. It was a sunny fall afternoon when Muffin crept down the sidewalk to Romeo's for a snack. Later that day, after he'd failed to return home, the students traced his usual route to the deli. No one had any information to offer. Muffin had vanished.

Back at the old Victorian, the students typed their lament on pale-green paper. They listed the date of the disappearance and wrote, "Muffin is a gray striped, very lovable male cat. He likes to sun himself on the sidewalk on Linden Street, and meet passersby. Muffin has a very distinctive meow. . . . If you have any information about him, please call . . ."

What was his "distinctive meow"? Was it funny or loud? A croak or a sonata?

It took an entire month for me to notice the poster hanging on the deli wall. It didn't shout at you like so many of the other posters I'd come across. The print was light, and without a photograph it lacked the instantaneously recognizable features of a lost-cat poster. After five years of sleuthing, I knew that an old poster could still be in play. I decided to call Muffin's owners.

One of the three college students who cared for Muffin spoke with me over the phone. Henry no longer anticipated Muffin's return. I asked him what he thought had happened. I heard his sigh over the phone. "Muffin never got over the death of Old Cat," he said. "Somehow, Muffin's sadness loosened his emotional ties to us. He must have followed a passerby home, and they took him in, and they love him like we did."

His fairy-tale ending caught me off guard. After I hung up the phone, I mused on his choice of words and thought about Zak, whose return home had been a fairy tale in itself—a late-night rescue from a neighbor's locked and empty house. Henry hadn't been given the chance to save his cat. By imagining that his cat was living the good life in a parallel universe, Henry's ending tapped into an age-old theme, the belief that the missing are given a chance to start life anew. In his secret world, Muffin was thriving. This was Henry's solace.

We hope for renewal in this life, or if not, at least in the beyond. I tried to imagine it, too—Muffin curled up on a couch on a nearby street, safe and loved. I wanted to believe it. Henry reminded me of Wuss's owner. She'd wanted her love to protect Wuss from the bully cat. Henry's love reached even further, beaming into an unknown world where Muffin hasn't lost anything. He's nourished and safe.

Henry's ending also reminded me of the last time I spoke with Holly about Eccles, four years earlier. She and Eccles would be reunited after she discovered how to find him, once again. Until that time, Eccles was safe, too, and simply wandering like his old self. I liked that. She and Henry believed in hope—the resurrection of love.

Muffin's disappearance coincided with a new client who offered a problem that I'd never encountered before and probably will not encounter again. Hope had become a torment for her.

"My father is gone," Sandra said at our first therapy session.

Her eyelids lingered on the downward blink and then sprung open.

"I'm sorry." Assuming it was a recent death I asked, "How did he die?"

"No," she said, closing her eyes. "He disappeared."

She was twenty-five years old and worked as a personal trainer at an exclusive gym. Two months earlier, her father, a divorced dad, stopped returning her calls. She was an only child, and at first, she wasn't sure how to interpret his silence. She described him as an unconventional, eccentric father whom she loved very much. He was a philosopher-artist who—despite having a substantial trust fund—lived frugally in a small studio. When Sandra was a girl, her father took her to the museums and parks in New York, generally nourishing the life of her mind. But he was less reliable when it came to providing steady meals or getting her to school on time.

"He liked to be alone," she said, "and he took off from time to time, but he would always call. My grandmother, who lives in Denver, has no idea where he is. She's hired a private detective."

As missing persons go, her father was difficult to track. He was average looking and financially independent, and he never used credit cards. He didn't drink nor did he take drugs, and he hadn't appeared on any hospital or police records. Her father could have traveled anywhere or simply vanished in New York City.

Three months went by. Sandra, fearing that her dad was dead or had fallen ill, felt helpless and abandoned. But once the belief took hold that she wasn't now and had never been important to her father, her grief became crushing. Had he started a new life?

Soon thereafter she began sleeping with a famous actor. "I fell in love with him," she said, effervescently. "We have great talks." Sandra's desire to be wanted overpowered the aspects of their "great talks" that weren't palatable to her. This famous actor liked, but didn't love her. The ups and downs of their love affair consumed her inside and outside of therapy.

About ten months later, when she realized the actor would continue to date other women, Sandra broke off the affair. Her grief became a catalyst toward seeing the ways she'd embellished her father-daughter relationship. In fact, the actor was similar to her father. He'd always been unreliable, but she preferred his passive manner to her mother's combative style. She used to plead with him to get a bigger apartment so that she could move in with him. He told her once, offhandedly, that he didn't want children. She was an accident. He said it the way you'd tell someone, "I have to go to the store now."

He might not speak to her for the entire day, and then spontaneously his mood would brighten. "I thought he was disappointed in me," Sandra recalled. "I used to read my book, try not to move or make a sound, and wait for him to talk again." At the age of sixteen, she ran away and worked as a waitress in Europe.

Slowly, Sandra began to realize that her childhood had been an extended attempt to normalize her father. Eccentric meant disturbed. In his own way, he loved her, but his capacity for connection was limited. She mourned the father she wished she'd had. Letting go of her image of him also allowed her to have compassion for herself. Her father didn't fathom that children, and even adults, needed emotional continuity in order to feel safe and loved. It seemed fair to say that in his mind, he'd never abandoned her.

Once Sandra stopped attributing emotions to her father that he didn't possess, she was freed from the fear that he'd left her because she was unlovable. She could stop longing for the home she was never going to have with the father she'd always loved. She could also stop longing for its modern equivalent: the commitment that the actor was never going to offer her.

With new clarity, Sandra got the loving parts of her father

back—the father who used to read to her, who taught her how to sketch and watercolor, the one who took her to Central Park and patiently taught her about botany and astronomy. She remembered the man who'd held on to her hand at the zoo, after the polar bear swam up from his underwater cave and scared her.

During therapy I often ask clients to imagine the core of their parents—what if they'd been able to live at their best, without battling their own flaws? When my clients can imagine their parents unmasked and undefended, seeing them for the people who wanted to love better than their parenting skills allowed, their shoulders relax, their breathing slows down. Freed of trying to fix the past, clients only have to fix their present.

A month later, Sandra's grandmother called. Her father was discovered living in a boarding house in Portland, Oregon. Sandra flew out to visit him. He was happy to see her, but he didn't understand what all the fuss was about. He liked the boarding house.

"We sat on this beat-up couch," she said tenderly, "and I cried and told him that I loved him and he said he loved me."

"The situation must have seemed . . . surreal?"

Her eyes said yes. "But I saw that he liked his world, and that he was safe. I was glad to get back on the plane and come back to my world, where I want to be."

Unlike Henry, who could only imagine Muffin's new world, Sandra had an opportunity to visit the land of missing loved ones. She'd been given a gift—the chance to see her father in his parallel universe.

Lost Dad,
found him,
the loves of a girl.

October 20

Zak has wandered away again and he took his tag off!!!

Our cat is missing <u>AGAIN</u>

Friendly, full-sized, male, neutered
Orange-Tabby Cat

Please call (203) 555-1333.

Characteristics of our loving cat:

A.   Loves food, travel, and people in the neighborhood

B.   Has thoroughly mastered the art of taking his collar off.

C.   Lives on State Street

D.   Tends to elude his cat-sitter when his parents go on vacation (i.e. last weekend).

E.   Makes direct eye-contact and seems hungry even though he has his own cat door and has known how

    to get in, eat his own food, and curl up wherever he likes. Nonetheless, curiosity continuously calls. .

Please return him to State Street or call (203) 555-1333.

ZAK, PART TWO

Zak lived his life like a wise guy in the mob. Down the street from the house, he had a tuna charge account at Amato's Italian Restaurant. His meals were served by the kitchen screen door. On Saturday nights, he hung with the bouncer at the local bar, and from the sidewalk they listened to the band. When the bar closed at 1 a.m., young, tipsy women would take out their cell phones and make me regret Zak's collar and tag. "Your kitty cat seems lost," they'd slur into the phone. "You should come get him. I'm at the bar here."

"Thanks, but he's not lost. That's where he hangs out on Saturday nights. He likes the music. He's safe, really. It's a one-way street."

"No, he's lost!" they'd insist, their voices rough from too many tequila shots. An instant later, the girls would deteriorate into sniffling sentimentality. "I don't want him to get run over." They'd get all weepy, and I'd stumble out of bed, throw on a jacket and clogs, and walk down the street. The goal was not to rescue Zak, but to shut the girls up so that I could get back to sleep and stop worrying about them doing something stupid, like taking him home.

In front of the bar and against his will, I'd scoop Zak up in my arms, but I'd always put him down two or three houses later. He liked his freedom. I knew he'd come home and be a family man when he was ready.

Zak liked just about everyone he met, but he also knew who had access to a can opener. What his paws lacked in dexterity, his mind overcompensated for in chicanery. He had a very convincing "hungry orphan" shtick. New Haven's a college town, so there are always new neighbors. He conned more than a few with his "I'm-homeless-please-feed-me" routine. Sometimes it went too far—not only would they feed him dinner, but breakfast as well.

Zak's incarceration was several years in the past and, after the neighbors had moved away, I never worried about the occasional all-night adventure. But his popularity was a problem. Strangers would often pet Zak when he was lying on the front porch steps. If they saw me they would say, "So this is where he lives?"

"Yup."

"He visits a lot. I live over there." They would point somewhere toward another street. "I fed him one night and he slept over. He's so sweet."

During one of his unauthorized sleepovers, Karis created a marketing plan—the Lost Cat "Laminated-for-Endurance" Personal Ad. She described it as a just-in-case-he-went-missing poster. We'd keep an arsenal of standbys in the house at all times, and since his seductive tricks would already be listed, all we'd have to do is change the dates as needed.

It wasn't long before we had a chance to test it out. Zak missed breakfast. Was he having brunch at another house? Had a do-gooder taken him in? Up went the signs. But just as we staple-gunned a poster on one side of the telephone pole, we saw a *found* poster on the other side, reading, ORANGE TABBY CAT—HUNGRY.

Apparently Zak was working his mojo again. He'd probably

appeared on someone's doorstep with a tin cup, meowing, "I'm blind. Feed me."

We hurried over to the address listed on the poster. Sure enough, not only had Zak showed up at some stranger's house, he'd strolled through an open porch door and up the stairs into a second-floor apartment. It belonged to a student with the laid-back look of a grunge band singer. He thought Zak was home-less because he'd lost his collar and was meowing a lot. The student mistook meowing for hunger pangs. He had no way of knowing that when Zak liked someone, he'd meow "hello" re-peatedly. But I also think we offer food because we feel pleasure upon meeting a person or an animal. We want to do something for them. ("Hungry? Sit down and eat! I insist.") Zak had a late dinner and a slumber party followed. And breakfast, too. The next day the *found* posters went up. Then I showed up, took him home, and placed him under house arrest.

It didn't bother Zak. In twenty-four hours, he'd be back on the streets, fleecing another soft-touch Yalie fresh from the Mid-west. But now we were prepared.

I'll never know if it was his nature or my nurture that made Zak so eager to be with people. If it was the luck of genes, then I was simply fortunate to have picked him. I like to think that my love and attention influenced him, too. I'd just started my doc-torate in psychology when I got him. He was six weeks old at the time, and I was taking a course on the theory of infant attach-ment. It's the study of how babies and toddlers learn to feel safe with their caretakers, so I decided to respond to Zak as if he were an infant. If he cried in the night and I heard him, I picked him up. If he wanted to snuggle on my throat, I let him, even if it interrupted my sleep. When he meowed to me, I meowed back. I don't know what I said, but he usually responded by rub-bing against my legs.

I cop to being a permissive parent, but I wanted Zak to feel confident and independent. When he was still small, I took him out for tree climbing. In the front of the house, he clawed up the trunk of a giant maple, but he climbed too high and was afraid to find his way down. I had to call my friend Judy and ask her to bring over a ladder. Then I climbed up with a piece of turkey in one hand and placed it on the branch so that Zak's little sniffer would smell the aroma and he'd want to learn how to turn around on the branch. When he got close enough to nibble the turkey I snatched him and down the ladder we went. He tried to lick my hand, the one smeared with turkey juice.

Every so often for the next couple of months, until he perfected his technique, I had to walk through the neighborhood and call "Zaky! Zaky!" until I heard a plaintive meow from atop a cluster of oak trees. Eventually he learned to come inside by climbing up to and banging on my bedroom window. I wasn't blindsided by love. Zak had true magnetism and I have proof from an impartial witness: My next-door neighbor, a pony-tailed hippie. Although we never talked, we had a solid relationship, based on nodding at each other in street. One afternoon, while I was sitting on my porch stoop, he stopped his bike and told me that he was moving. "Is it all right if I come back and visit?" My thoughts rushed toward confusion. Then he added, "You know . . . visit Zak. He's such a great cat! He comes over and we hang out every day." I wondered if there were going to be visitation hassles and custody hearings, but it worked out.

Zak may have been friendly, but he was still discriminating. He liked to beat up big dogs. I tried to warn a lady who was walking toward my house holding her German Shepherd on a leash. From my porch, I yelled to her, "My cat attacks dogs. You might want to cross the street." She looked at my thirteen-pound cat resting on the sidewalk and then at her seventy-pound killing machine. Unfazed, she continued her march toward destruction. Zak either smelled or heard the intruder and woke in a fury. Suddenly, he was airborne, flying straight into the dog. He slapped the dog on the face with his left paw. The Shepherd yelped, and faster than a speeding bullet in reverse, he retreated. The dog dragged his owner into my neighbor's yard. After they composed themselves, the dog and his owner crossed the street. Zak resumed his nap.

Some milestones in life are easy to identify: graduating, moving, beginning or ending a relationship, the death of family or friends. Then there are the subtle markers of time, the ones we only recognize in hindsight, because we were too busy living when they occurred. We didn't realize that people and places and pets demarcated eras of our lives that would always be linked through memory. Remembering one part of an era, other memories will spring to life. A cat can forge that link.

My years with Zak turned had turned into decades. My practice in New York flourished and for two years Karis and I continued to split our time between New Haven and the city. I left the bedroom window open so that Zak could climb the pine tree and come and go as he pleased, so that he could still have his freedom, friends, and neighborhood capers. I knew how miserable he would have been trapped inside a small apartment in the city. Still, to make sure that Zak wouldn't feel abandoned, I asked a friend to move into the guest bedroom. For two years, Karis, Zak, and I carried on. Zak seemed to be his old self.

During one of my homecomings, I watched him saunter in from the sidewalk. I rubbed his neck and then went upstairs to unpack. Karis stayed with him on the porch. A minute later, I heard her yell, "Zaky can't get up the tree." I looked out the window and saw that he was halfway up the trunk and straining to hold on. His claws were dug in. His forearms seemed stalled. I called out to him and he looked up. "Zaky," I continued to call him. In case he fell, Karis remained next to the tree, standing underneath him. With us cooing encouragement he finally willed himself up to the top. It was his last climb.

The vet was well-meaning and, believing that Zak would

respond, tried an assortment of treatments for several weeks. I believed that he would improve, too. Zak had long defied the average eight-year mortality rate for outdoor cats. He was sixteen. But actuarial tables didn't matter to me. In my mind, Zak was going to live until at least twenty.

While I was working in New York, I spoke to the vet daily. He was waiting for the medications to work their magic. I felt relieved that Zak was in a cat hospital, safe and protected. Maybe he was a few naps away from getting back to his old routines. On weekends we visited him in the hospital. But on the third weekend, when I picked him up and felt his fragile body in my arms, I felt horror streak through my heart. Zaky was fading from this life.

I took him home. Karis and I had the weekend with him. He let me hold him as much as I wanted to. At one point, I left him with Karis and went downstairs to the kitchen, but she yelled out to me, "Zak's ears are moving as if he's following you through the house." I came back and held him again; he lifted his paw onto my face. It was good-bye. I told him, "Zak, it's okay to go."

It might have been two minutes or ten that I continued to hold him. I don't know. I only know that I looked into his eyes until he stopped breathing. I'd never been present at the moment when breath permanently ceased. When it was over, I couldn't speak. I couldn't even look away. Death had no solace. Only time, and I couldn't wait that long. And I couldn't release him from my arms.

Then something strange happened. Within seconds, Zak began to look younger. He changed shape and tone. His body softened. He felt lighter in my arms. The color of his fur seemed to shift, too, from faded and worn to a shiny orange. The light in his yellow eyes turned radiant. When the last calendar page stopped turning back, Zak was no longer his adult self. He was

Zaky the adolescent kitty of tree-climbing age. I loved seeing his radiance, but how could his youthful appearance be real?

But I wasn't alone. Karis saw it, too. Zak's spirit had morphed his body back to its essence. This was solace. We'd remember Zak as he'd lived—as an especially vibrant and happy cat.

Later, we went into the backyard to bury Zak in the meditation garden. He'd liked to hide there. In the center were tall sea grasses surrounded by tiger lilies. A small concrete statue of the standing Buddha, representing happiness, was front and center. As we dug the grave, I could feel Zak in my heart, but also *on* my heart. It wasn't an ephemeral emotion or longing. It was a solid feeling of knowing that he was here in another form. I learned a truth about dying that I would never lose—bodies come and go. Spirit lives. Solaced by Zak, I could feel my mother, sister, and father, too.

I felt his weight and warmth on my chest. Three days later, while I was sitting on a bench in the garden and remembering how the sun would streak across his face when he hid in the leaves, I felt his presence suddenly vanish. I didn't say anything to Karis, because I thought it was best to let her have her own timetable of mourning. Another three days later, I hinted by saying that Zak felt far away.

"I know," she said. "He left three days ago." No longer ill or imprisoned by his body, Zak's spirit had reached back to its source. We thanked him for having taken the long way home.

"Are you going to get a new cat?" a client asked me a month later.

"I'm not ready yet," I answered.

"When you think about it," she mused, "if you lose your grandmother, no one says, 'When are you going to get a new one?'"

"Grieving and time," I told her, "will pick a new cat for me."

It was true, I needed time. The grace of Zak's death was a

treasured memory, but I felt frozen with guilt about the months leading up to his death. I left him alone.

Several months later, Karis and I sold the house and moved to New York full-time. I rented an office in New Haven, reversing my commute, and returned every week to see my clients.

Living in a fast-paced city like New York helped to dim the daily reminders of Zak. But while I treasured his last transcendent moments, I replayed them less and less, and instead I was haunted by my feelings of betrayal. Would he have become sick if I'd remained in New Haven? Did he die feeling that I'd abandoned him? That I'd left him to pursue a "lifestyle"? I wasn't there during his last weeks on earth. Some days I wished I believed in absolution, but I was the only one who could make peace with myself. I needed time, but not for mourning. Whenever I missed him I felt lousy about myself. And without realizing it, I tried not to think of Zak at all.

Every now and then, Karis would make a few references to the old days, but they spilled forth spontaneously. Without having to ask, she knew why I could barely speak about him.

But my friends and clients were still curious. "Are you going to get another cat?" I'd sigh and cut the conversation short. "Our apartment is too small," I'd answer, grateful to have avoided even saying his name. In retrospect I can say, "For God's sake, I'm a psychotherapist. Could I have really believed that I didn't deserve another cat?" Yes. Shame and grief gripped me.

I went about my routines. I looked the same. I went to work. I met friends. Only I took a break from collecting lost-cat posters. I didn't want to think about cats.

Then, about six months later a lost-cat poster collected *me*.

HAVE YOU SEEN
ME? I'M A BLACK
& WHITE KITTEN
3½ mos. OLD w/
GREEN HARNESS,
I WAS STOLEN
FROM PENN STATION
ALONG w/ A BLUE
& WHITE TWEED
BAG ON WHEELS.
PLEASE RETURN
TO HOMELESS
MARY

MARY

A wet snow was falling on Homeless Mary's lost-kitten poster, and her message, written in black magic marker, was already splotchy on the page. I shot a glance at the evening traffic, crawling by in the steady sleet. While the cars blocked the intersection, I waited on the curb and read the poster. It had no contact information—no phone number, no address, no specific location where the owner could be found. How, exactly, could the public help? I shuddered. "Homeless Mary" had become her name, address, and identity, all in one.

I pulled my hood forward to keep the sleet from landing on my glasses, and I pictured Mary's three-and-a-half-month-old kitten, tucked into the tweed bag. If Mary's cart was missing, not only had she lost her pet, but all her worldly possessions, too. And though her world didn't hold very much in it, after an hour's worth of slush it wouldn't even include her lost-cat poster. I took it down from the pole and folded it into my bag. I would hang it again when the storm passed.

I trudged toward home. It was cold and dark, and I was tired. I arrived at my apartment on Eighth Avenue, near Penn Station, and after I dried off and made some tea, I put the poster on the kitchen counter and studied it. I bore into the words, trying to extract more than Mary had intended. Her handwriting was neat and boldly printed, but slanted. She used fully formed sentences, complete with punctuation. Not bad for a handwritten sign, but overall it left me feeling claustrophobic. Even the empty spaces bothered me. They were blank, as I imagined her life to be. It was a stark plea from a helpless person.

When Karis came home, I showed her the poster. She grimaced. "Too close," she said, turning away. How could I have been so thoughtless? Karis had grown up homeless, before it turned into the national calamity it is now. In the 1970s, her unmedicated schizophrenic mother used to wake Karis and her sister in the middle of the night and usher them out of their apartment, never to return for clothes or toys or identification. They slept in bus stops, train stations, strange hippie apartments, and all-night diners.

During the more stable periods, Karis slept in the closet, cushioned by the dirty laundry. After she turned seven, the state intervened and sent the girls away to live with their father, an ex-military man and a religious fanatic. He married four times and had more children than he wanted or was able to take care of. By the time Karis was twelve years old, she was regularly jumping in between his fist and her six-year-old half brother. At eighteen, Karis left home. Leaving her younger siblings behind was the most difficult decision she'd ever made.

Meeting Karis turned my intellectual life upside down—I no longer knew what I believed about nature versus nurture. She had an innate sense of empathy. She also had a short fuse (mainly while driving or dealing with frustrating telephone recordings that never offered helpful options), but she was consistently fairminded and kind. "I always had this thing about integrity," she once said. "My crazy mother was better than my evil father. At least she wasn't actually trying to hurt me."

"You're brilliant," I told her repeatedly. I marveled at her old soul and inner wisdom. It was important to me that her current life be as reasonably happy as possible. She, in turn, offered me a rare experience. She deciphered my complexities and contradictions. I felt known and understood.

"When I was thirteen, I decided to run away," she told me. "I got a Greyhound bus schedule. It was five hours to Los Angeles, but then I figured that in five hours I'd be a child prostitute. So I didn't go." Karis didn't like to speak about her childhood.

"I shouldn't have surprised you with the poster," I said. "I'm sorry."

"Don't worry about it," she said from across the room. "I'm going to play Spider Solitaire."

I turned back to the poster, which was written from the vantage point of the kitten. *Have you seen me?* I couldn't help but wonder—was Mary also speaking for herself? Calling yourself "Homeless Mary" is about as invisible as you can get in New York. Why? When did she cross from one life into another?

I guessed that since she put the poster up near Madison Square Garden, she probably rested at night close-by, but I tried to imagine her before she'd lost her home. Was she one of the refugees fleeing the collapse of affordable housing in New York City? It's a familiar story. The city's tax incentives fueled the end of single-room-occupancy hotels and reasonably priced apartments. In their place, developers built luxury rentals and office buildings. After the destruction of the original Penn Station in the 1960s, the redesigned structure was jammed underground, and Madison Square Garden landed on top of it. While Penn Station became a transportation hub, an unanticipated second hub developed for the homeless.

I wanted to find Mary and tell her that I was sorry about the loss of her cat. I wanted to pass along the support that I'd been surprised to receive, mostly from strangers, who'd left messages of concern after finding my own lost-cat posters. I even fantasized about getting her a new kitten. If she wanted one, that is.

Living in an apartment near Penn Station, I encounter dozens of homeless people every day. I recognize the regulars, but sometimes I'm so tired of being panhandled that I get brusque. I had something to offer Mary, though, and it wasn't just spare change; it was respect. If Mary wanted money, she could have that, too.

Most of the regulars on my block had a routine, and I was hoping that Mary had one, too. How else was I supposed to find her? After the morning rush, I stopped outside of Penn Station and asked the other homeless people, "Have you seen Mary?"

It was a chilly, sunny day, and a middle-aged woman who looked like a stocky, suburban mom stood next to a trash can near the 34th Street subway platform. Donna's brown hair was mashed under a navy-blue ski cap, which was folded over like a floppy bunny's ear. She wore several sweaters underneath a dirty, unzipped jacket. She was glad, she told me, that I'd approached her.

"I was feeling lonely today and wanted somebody to talk to." While she rocked from one foot to the other, Donna volunteered the underpinnings of her current status. She couldn't stop drinking. She used to be a teacher. She'd been fighting with her abusive boyfriend and gone back on the street so that he couldn't find her. "It's important to know where the clean public bathrooms are," she said, leaning forward. "McDonald's is a good one."

Donna didn't know Mary, and I started to leave. She followed me, and her speech grew more frantic. "Don't go yet," she said. I tried to put a dollar in her Styrofoam cup, but she stopped me. There was beer in it.

I had conversations with other homeless people, like the young man collecting cans from the garbage container. He wore a tattered green parka with the hood pulled forward until his face was completely framed. He was shy and soft-spoken, and he lived under the 23rd Street subway platform. He didn't know Mary.

There had to be a better way.

I asked the police in Penn Station for help. The officers in the information booth were assigned by Homeland Security, but they only knew about the small area that they guarded. They didn't understand the entire complex layout of the station, and they had no idea where the homeless lived. They wore green-and-black fatigues that must have worked well in Vietnam, but in the urban jungle, asphalt-colored camouflage with potholes would have been more effective. They shooed me away and pointed me toward the "Lost and Found."

The Lost and Found office in Penn Station is small, gray, and windowless. When I walked in, the fluorescent lighting held the room hostage with a bright, jaundiced, migraine-inducing glow. Like a thrift store, it was overflowing with coat racks and shelves piled high with forgotten backpacks, luggage, books, and radios. Shoes, too. (I guess a few commuters were socking around New York City.) Of course, there wasn't a spot for lost animals, and no one had turned in a kitten.

Charles, a tall, handsome, African American man with a deep baritone voice, ran the Lost and Found. He was relaxed and soft-spoken.

"There's a bunch of random stuff here," I said, pointing to his overcrowded desk, where dozens of pairs of eyeglasses lay waiting for the nearsighted to claim them.

"If we find it, nobody calls," he shrugged. "If we don't, the people call every day."

Charles knew Mary.

"She comes at different times, every day, looking for her cat." Almost apologetically, he added, "I don't think the cat is real." I didn't understand what he meant.

"It's in her imagination," he said.

"She made a poster for an *imaginary* kitten?" I didn't know what to believe. "Why would she do that?"

"A lot of the homeless make stuff up," Charles said. "They

can't help it. It's in their head, but it's not real. The bag was probably stolen, but with a cat inside of it? I don't think so." He knew several Penn Station locals who kept dogs for companionship, but he didn't know anyone who had a cat. "A cat is a whole different thing," he said. "It's not as easy. They wander." He added, "Dogs don't."

I wasn't prepared for the plot twist. I felt unsettled. All of my assumptions were under strain, but still he knew about Mary.

Initially, after her kitten was "stolen," Mary would walk into the Lost and Found and ask, "Did anyone turn in my kitty?" Charles didn't have to look up when Mary entered the office. "She was ripe," he said. "She lights up a room."

The news of her poor hygiene was a grim poke and a reminder. I was caught between my gestures of middle-class compassion and the reality of poverty. I wasn't naïve, I'd grown up in several subcultures simultaneously. We lived in the suburbs, but my father taught school in the inner city, and I spent my summers in the inner city parks. I'd been the director of a battered woman's shelter in Bridgeport, Connecticut. I'd talked abusive men into tears and had others arrested. I wasn't averse to grit. But I wanted Mary to be in less dire straits.

Charles said that as the weeks went by, Mary stopped coming into the office. Instead, she stood behind the door and opened it just enough to peek in. He'd shake his head, and she'd say, "Thank you," and then she'd leave. He didn't know where she stayed at night or when she was going to show up next.

I'd hoped that with a good physical description of Mary I'd be able to track her down. Charles guessed that she was in her forties, but he wasn't sure, because her face had a street look—tired and dirty. She had a ruddy Irish complexion and appeared to be overweight, but she was layered in mismatched coats and sweaters, so it was tough to say.

If Charles was right, Homeless Mary was psychotic and

searching for an imaginary cat. If he was wrong, she was still searching for a cat that she'd probably never find.

Hallucinations and delusions have an inner logic to the person experiencing them, and the more effective psychotherapists are willing to explore the significance of their clients' delusions. Years ago, a colleague of mine who worked in an emergency room began an interview with a homeless woman who appeared to be terrified. When asked her name, the woman remained silent for a minute, and then whispered, "I don't have a name. Someone stole it." Her delusional speak was perfectly descriptive. She didn't feel real.

Mary knew her own name, and she'd even elaborated on it. "Homeless Mary" defined herself by what she *didn't* possess, and that truth defined everything else in her life.

Real or not, Mary's cat meant something to her—perhaps someone to love, or someone to love her, or maybe it was a memory of a happier time. We will never know. As the winter months pressed on, I'd occasionally stop homeless women in Penn Station and ask if they knew Mary. Sometimes, out on the street, her imperfect physical description knocking around in my head, I'd ask a woman if her name was Mary. It never was, and I was always surprised at the subtle sense of relief I felt. I didn't have to face the futility of it all head on. I didn't have to make it real just yet. I'd already anticipated the sadness I'd feel when it was over and I had to say good-bye.

After five years of sleuthing, I'd discovered the darkest story. Nancy Drew was grieving. It was six months after Zak's death, but I didn't consciously know that. I only knew that Zak was gone. It was winter. I lived in New York and Mary's cat poster broke my heart.

While searching for Mary up and down Eighth Avenue, it seemed to me like my neighborhood was the crowded city of

Calcutta. I was bombarded by the class systems. The wealthy Brahmins, the middle class, the tourists, the poor, and the untouchables, all traveling on the same sidewalks but arriving at a different station in life. This is the challenge of living in New York. Class is an underlying influence. I don't like myself when I'm irritable, particularly when it's toward people who have less than I do. I know better.

It was a bleak winter. I always seemed to be recovering from the flu. Some weeks, instead of walking to work, I had to take a cab. Still, after two months of intermittently searching for Mary I fantasized about an old-fashioned stakeout where I'd cancel the day's sessions and roam around Penn Station. But it seemed over the top. Besides, I despised Penn Station. It's an underground shopping tomb filled with crummy chain stores. The ceilings are too low and it's noisy. The foot traffic comes at you from all directions and like all crypts it's short on breathable air. Besides, I wasn't fooling myself. It mattered to *me* if I met Mary. Not to her.

I went back to see Charles. He'd last seen Mary about two weeks earlier. She was still looking for her kitten, but her visits had dropped off. He thought she might have given up. The kitten remained imaginary.

He sat at his desk and I put my shoulder bag down on the floor and engaged him in a half-hearted debate. I pointed out that Mary's poster was fairly specific—the kitten was black and white, three-and-a-half-months old, and wearing a green harness. "I saw a homeless lady on Fifth Avenue who had a metal grocery store cart," I said, "and instead of a little kid sitting in the front seat, there was a cat. He had a harness."

"I've been here for twenty-eight years, Nancy," Charles said patiently. "You have to understand, when people go off their medication, they remember stuff, but it could be from their childhood. There was this woman who for twenty years walked around looking for 'Richard.' Day after day, she'd step up to the passengers, and even the employees, and say, 'I'm looking for Richard. He went to Washington, D.C. When's he coming back?' She looked like a middle-class lady. Her hair was done and she had fresh clothes. People tried to help. They gave her money, too. Then she disappeared. A lot of the time you see somebody for years and then one day they're gone and you don't know why."

He thought Mary had been hallucinating. Maybe she'd had a break with reality. Maybe she'd had a kitten when she was a little girl.

"How'd she keep a cat inside a bag?" he asked me.

I realized that each time she'd stuck her head through the Lost and Found door, Mary had asked Charles about her kitty and not about her missing possessions. Details like this kept me unsure. But I couldn't help from leaning toward believing her.

"It's difficult to know what's real," Charles said. "Some of the homeless have developed ruses or fake identities to enhance their standing among the other homeless. There was a homeless man who used to wear a priest's outfit," he said, shaking his head. "A cop told me the truth. So, Mary's got a lot of company."

Charles eventually shared a story about himself. When he was thirteen, his father, a New York cop, drove his kids to the Bowery. At the time, it was known as Skid Row, where the drunks collapsed together after they'd ruined their lives. His father pointed out of the window at the winos lying on the sidewalk and said, "You drop out of school, this is what happens."

Charles told me that years earlier, before the city had tightened its restrictions, the homeless had openly slept on the floor of Penn Station. Eventually, some of them moved into hiding spots within the maze of the old building, part of which is still standing inside the new Penn Station. There was a group of teenagers from a nearby welfare hotel who lived in a condemned bathroom until they were in their mid-twenties. "They knew the ins and outs of Penn Station better than anyone," Charles said. "I watched them grow up." Then he added, "For a woman who's all by herself, Mary might want a place that's not so isolated."

Three months had passed since I'd first seen Mary's poster, and the weather was getting warmer. Charles told me that Mary's appearance had changed. She seemed thinner, but she might have been trying to protect herself during the winter by wearing bulky clothes that made her look bigger. In the springtime, she wore a dirty red raincoat. Her hair seemed blonder, and she'd replaced her stolen blue-and-white tweed cart on wheels with a small metal laundry cart.

Our conversation was interrupted by a traveler who came in looking for his briefcase—he'd left it on a train in the overhead compartment. While Charles helped him, I continued leaning on the counter. I decided to give up completely on the idea of finding Mary. Maybe it was a rationalization, but I accepted that meeting her would only haunt me, and now I was questioning what I actually had to offer her.

I wanted Mary to have a real cat, in part because it would have normalized her—instead of suffering from psychosis and homelessness, she'd suffer from only one of them. I wanted her to have companionship and someone to look after. A life other than her own that needed her. I wanted to know if the cat was real, of course, but I'd also wanted to commiserate with her.

What if I changed my vantage point and tried to understand Mary's belief system? Like the delusional woman who believed that her name had been stolen, Mary's search for a missing cat might have been symbolic of something else. She'd lost something important and was asking for help. Whether or not the kitten was imaginary, Mary had gone through the same paces as other lost-cat owners—searching, hanging posters, and relying on her neighbors for assistance. Without a permanent home or other resources, and maybe even without all of her faculties, the Lost and Found was Mary's only stable address. Her posters were hanging near the train station because that really was her neighborhood. Whatever I believed, her black-and-white kitten with a green harness was gone. In the end, Mary was just like me and the other owners. She was bereft.

The man who'd come looking for his briefcase left disappointed, and I was about to do the same, disheartened for my own reasons.

"What do you think Mary's real story is?"

"You just can't tell," Charles said. "Most of the time, the homeless don't want you to know, and they don't want their families to know how far they have fallen."

"And Mary?"

"We'll never know how much she's lost."

MISSING!

Bailey

PLEASE HELP US!

Reward!

Persian Himalayan, white, long hair
flat nose & face. She's small & 1 yr old.

Call (651) 555-4789

Her family misses her so much.
Please bring her home.

BAILEY

There's a Buddhist parable about luck. A poor farmer is given a beautiful horse. The neighbors say that he is lucky. The farmer says, "It could be good luck or bad luck, we shall see." The farmer's son falls off the horse and breaks his leg.

The neighbors say, "Bad luck now."

The farmer says, "Could be good luck, could be bad, we shall see."

The emperor's army sweeps through the town and conscripts all the able-bodied young men. The son is left behind.

The neighbors say, "Good luck now."

"Could be good luck, could be bad, we shall see," the farmer says.

The family cat vanishes.

The neighbors say, "Bad luck now."

The farmer says, "We shall see."

One evening the phone rang, and the woman on the other end of the line said that'd she'd gotten my number from an online chat room for lost-cat owners. I was flabbergasted. I don't seek employment as a sleuth on the Internet, nor do I advertise my limited skill set—nosiness and a fondness for whiskers and tails. How had she heard of me?

Turns out I had Holly to thank. Montana Maddy's owner!

"How's she doing?"

"Quite well . . . she actually gave me your number ages ago, but I never called."

"Did she ever find Maddy?"

"No, unfortunately, but she told me that you'd found your cat by calling a psychic. If I'm not intruding, would it be okay to get your psychic's number?"

Maybe I *should* have been advertising—WWW.CATPOSTER SLEUTH.COM. EMPATHY GUARANTEED.

Jamie's story was filled with layers of mystery. She was willing to go to extraordinary lengths to find her cat Bailey, including making three different lost-cat poster templates. After we spoke, she sent all of them to me. A year earlier, Jamie had been in her backyard when she had run inside to answer the phone. At some point during the next three minutes, Bailey, one of her two white long-haired Himalayan kittens, squeezed through a slatted fence and out of sight. At first, Jamie and her partner searched on foot. By the time midnight tolled, they were driving through their Massachusetts suburban neighborhood, high beams flashing.

She caught a glimpse of white fur on the side of the road. They jumped out of the car, leaving it rumbling in the middle of the street with the headlights on. Jamie waved her flashlight and ran toward her kitten shouting, "Bailey, Bailey!" He ran, too, but not into her arms. Bailey disappeared into the woods.

"I ruined my chance," she said. "I was new to cats. I should have been calm and approached him slowly."

Several nights later, two neighbors heard meowing, and when they turned on their porch lights, both of them saw a white cat scurry into the bushes. But Jamie hadn't learned about the additional sightings until the following year—her neighbors never reported them. Inertia, not malice, was the cause. But that's not the mystery, either.

Once Jamie realized how difficult it would be to rescue Bailey, she masterminded a multimedia campaign, which started out with a lost-cat poster pumped up on steroids. Earlier that year, a professional photographer had taken portraits of Bailey and her identical twin sister.

"I had Bailey's photographs blown up until they were three feet long, and then I laminated them onto plywood," she told me, with subdued pride. She staked six of them into the ground near the exits and entrances of what she described as her nouveau riche neighborhood.

Next, she Xeroxed seven hundred flyers and stuffed them in her neighbors' mailboxes. She also put an ad in the paper. "A friend gave me a one-time spot on a local cable show," Jamie said, "and I offered a five-hundred-dollar reward for Bailey's return. But no luck."

Still, Jamie's publicity campaign had an immediate impact. Someone knocked her giant posters to the ground, and after she put them back up, they were knocked down all over again. Determined to win the battle, if not the war, she bought aircraft cables to hold them in place, but someone cut the cables and stole four of the posters. In the evenings, she received anonymous phone calls from a man who whimpered, "*Meow*, I'm cold, I'm hungry."

It was mean-spirited and immature, but to be perfectly honest, I felt like laughing. I found it to be perversely funny—black humor from someone who I assumed was annoyed by her publicity campaign. I wondered about my own reaction, which was probably an indirect response to her King Kong-sized posters. They pushed aside the public's natural empathy for a missing cat and made you wonder: "Who the hell *is* this woman?"

The man harassed Jamie's household every night for several months. According to the phone company he used a pay phone.

One day while Jamie was standing in the yard a man drove by. "I'm sick and tired of your fucking posters," he yelled. "I want to hurt you." She called the state police twice (there was no local police department), but both times troopers refused to run the license plate through their computer system because they needed "special paperwork" from their supervisor. Finally, on her third call, another trooper ran the report. The car belonged to an elderly man who was known to be unstable. He was the anonymous caller, too. "He was such an unhappy person," Jamie said, and she refused to press charges.

The old man wasn't the only one taking umbrage with the skyscraper-tall, lost-cat posters. "The neighbors wanted me to take them down," she said, in a matter-of-fact tone.

The more we spoke, the more uncertain I became of my attitude toward Jamie's behavior. She was clearly aggrieved, but not vindictive or loose with accusations or blame. She seemed to sincerely contemplate my questions before answering.

"Did you realize that people wouldn't want to drive past posters of that size every day?" I asked.

"I was desperate to find Bailey, and nobody read the little posters," she said. Her brief explanation seemed reasonable to me during the flurry of our conversation. The garish publicity campaign continued despite her neighbors' protests.

"How did you handle being harassed, ignored by the police, and disliked by your neighbors?"

"In spite of everything," she said, "I still feel that people are basically good inside, though everyone has their problems." Before Bailey vanished, Jamie had a morning routine, which included daily meditation, prayer, and reading books about spirituality. With a dry laugh, she told me it might have been wise to notify St. Francis of Assisi, patron saint of animals.

"Perhaps you should have invested in a garden statue of him, the kind with the little critters at his feet?"

"And placed it next to the fence so that he could call Bailey home," Jamie said, but the lightness in her voice yielded to her more formidable yearnings.

This time, her rich spiritual life remained separate from the growing feelings of depression. "Even when close family members had died," Jamie said, "I felt profound grief, but not depression. Losing Bailey was somehow different. I couldn't shake it. Friends wanted me to go on antidepressants."

"Did you consider it?"

"I thought it was the beginning of a deep inner sadness. I knew I had to go through it."

I considered her predicament. Did her symptoms meet the criteria for moderate depression—sadness, poor concentration, despair, irritability, and so forth—or did her moderate depression meet the criteria for the vicissitudes of life and the melancholy that comes with transition, loss of innocence, personal change, and grief? I understood her reluctance to try medication. For her it wasn't an authentic solution. She wanted to discover the depth of her sorrow and resilience.

She concentrated on her work as a sound specialist for a media company, but her search continued. Bailey was in the neighborhood. She sensed it, and she grew increasingly desperate to find him. Friends had pushed her to speak with a local psychic. I was surprised to hear it, given the pretext of her call. Did she need a second psychic's opinion or was it a burst of activity all in the wrong direction? Jamie filled in the backstory.

Before she proceeded with a full reading, Jamie tested the psychic's acumen. Would she be able to describe Bailey's appearance? After passing the test, the psychic offered a remarkably detailed description of one house in particular, as well as the people who lived there. Jamie was stunned: It was her neighbor's house. And Jamie's eight-year-old nephew played on the same soccer team as the woman's son. Jamie didn't hesitate. She marched over and knocked on their door. The mother admitted to seeing Bailey in their yard a month earlier.

"He looked hungry," she said, and her weasel eyes blinked. "But he ran away and I don't know anything else. I wish I did."

Jamie felt light-headed. The mother was lying. She knew it. Bailey was a sweet lap cat, easy to fall in love with. He was inside their house. Hidden from sight. Of course, the family had seen the lost-cat signs. At six feet tall, astronauts could have seen the posters from outer space. Why wouldn't she have told Jamie of the sighting? There was only one explanation: Her neighbor had *stolen* Bailey.

Jamie walked home feeling like she'd taken a punch to the solar plexus. She couldn't breathe. Her feelings changed with every step—joy, fear, disgust, bewilderment, helplessness, relief. She could fill the alphabet. But one thought above all others consumed her: How would she get stolen Bailey back?

She asked Animal Control for guidance. "We only deal with dogs," they said. "And besides, do you have any proof?" Ownership is difficult to establish, even with photographs. The police are likely to say it's a civil matter, not criminal. Unless it's breaking and entering, they generally don't get involved in neighbor and property disputes.

After much brooding and soul-searching, Jamie decided to approach her neighbor's kids. She worried about putting them in the middle of an argument, but if she could assume a casual approach, it would be relatively harmless. Maybe they'd reveal something of value. She just needed to be easygoing.

By three o'clock the next afternoon, she felt nauseous. She went to pick up her nephew at the bus stop and asked both of her neighbor's children, "How's it going?"

They said, "Okay," with typical, childlike shyness.

"How's your new cat?" she said stiffly.

"Uh . . ." Both the son and daughter stammered and looked down at the ground. Neither was lifting up a chin. Not even to say, "He's okay."

"I changed the subject," Jamie said, guilt-stricken. Instead, she asked them about the school soccer game. "They looked so unhappy. I think they were told not to say anything about having a new cat." Jamie was livid at the mother. Stealing her cat was one transgression. Asking her children to lie was another. Allowing Jamie to suffer was the third. But it all paled in comparison to a broader crime. The mother held a position of public trust. She was a pediatrician. "She shouldn't be around children." Jamie raised her voice at the good universe, the one she was used to believing in. It was starting to crack.

Bailey's whereabouts became undeniable. During the next few months, several of her friends saw Bailey's white face in the living room window of the doctor's house. Jamie, of course, frequently drove by. She saw Bailey in a side window on three separate occasions.

I got up from my chair. I needed to walk around while we spoke. If I believed that my neighbors had kidnapped Zak, and then denied it, my rage would take over. Anger would seethe. Injustice would howl. Vengeance would be mine.

But what did Jamie do? She hung more posters up on the telephone poles near the doctor's house. "I was hoping the family would break," she said. "I was hoping that goodwill would finally prevail. Some of my friends told me to break in while the family was gone, but I was too afraid." She remained hopeful that she could rescue her cat without breaking the law.

The winter months were taxing. Every few weeks, she saw Bailey in the window. She confronted the family again and heard the same denials. Jamie said, "I don't get it. Why steal Bailey? They could get their own white cat."

When summer rolled around, Bailey had been "missing" for nine months. Of course, most people had no idea that he'd been stolen and was living nearby. A friend of Jamie's who worked at a local store overheard a group of mouthy teenagers making fun of the heartbroken owner. One teenage girl went so far as to call Jamie's house and leave a message. "I saw a coyote eat a ball of

fluff, so stop looking," she said. "Your cat's dead." Jamie spoke
to the girl's mother, who didn't seem to think her daughter's
behavior was a problem.

I understood why. After a year of Jamie's searching, her neighbors were sick of the damn cat. (*"Give it up already!"*) But it didn't
excuse anyone's bad behavior.

"You don't need a second psychic's opinion," I said, finally
weighing in with the majority. "The first psychic told you what
you needed to know." Jamie remained quiet. "Perhaps your
friends were right. You have to find a way to get into the house."

"I don't know how," she said.

"You watch the house, and when it's empty, you go in and get
your cat."

If Jamie had misgivings about breaking the law, I understood
her reluctance, but she wasn't saying that was the source of her
hesitation. "I don't know how to get inside," she repeated. I
wondered if it was a question of will.

"You need courage." I was planting the idea for future use,
because today, the warrior inside of her was dormant.

"I'm going to wait and see if there's another way to get
Bailey."

Saying good-bye to Jamie while in a steadfast state of limbo
was difficult for me. Her story stayed with me for months. The
unfairness, the sense of betrayal, the loss of innocence, and her
own resistance to fighting mano a mano for her cat were threads
that had to be ripping the fabric of her life. With Zak gone, I was
avoiding the rips in my own.

Speaking with her while she stood on the precipice of her
cat's recovery helped me to understand why some owners may
have a better chance at finding their cats than others. Temperament, lifestyle, one's own stage of personal growth, even
experience as a pet owner—all of it converges and affects the
decision-making process. The variables become "the team," so
to speak, and the team examines the circumstances of the cat's

disappearance. As data is ruled in or out, the team reevaluates the ongoing strategy.

Some months later, my anecdotal ideas on how to find Bailey were confirmed. I called an 800 number listed on a lost-cat poster that I'd found in New York, and I accidentally discovered the author who wrote the book (at least the first book) on how to search for a missing pet. He answered the phone by saying, "Sherlock Bones, tracer of missing pets." *Did I hear that correctly?* Unless you're counting the movie *Ace Ventura,* I'd never heard of a real-life pet detective. Honestly, I didn't know you could subcontract the job. In fact, art had imitated life. He was a pet detective to the stars. He'd found Jim Carrey's non-celluloid dog. As we spoke, John, aka Sherlock Bones, explained his procedures, and I saw the similarities between our professions. We're both assessing our client's capacity to reach their goals. "For the missing cat, I create a psychological profile, the same way you would for a missing person," he explained. "I learn about the cat's temperament, routines, likes, and dislikes. You also want to know how the cat deals with stress, and different types of stress, too. Of course, I look at the disappearance itself—the circumstances, the details, the weather, the geography, the traffic patterns, and so on."

He should have charged for every wise word, but his fee was only $150 for a consult, with unlimited follow-up calls. "Sometimes clients take my advice," John said. "Sometimes they don't. Who knows why? I can help you expand upon what you're already doing. I build your luck up by adding experience to it."

This sounded like my experience with my own clients, too. Some of them are reluctant to follow my advice. They associate it, and sometimes me, with pain. But why buck the pet detective? Listen to his suggestions, based on thirty years of experience, and you get Spot or Fluffy back.

"I profile the owners, too," John said. "I have to. How else can I make a realistic plan if I don't know their capabilities or how available and motivated they are to search? Sometimes you have to help the client help themselves."

That's my job, too. John and I gauge how our clients react to our counsel. What feelings of fear, courage, or curiosity arise?

I've always believed that wherever there is personal truth, energy follows. If you really, truly want to do something, you become energized. Jamie's heart was filled with longing, but her hands and feet pawed at the same spot on the ground. Unfortunately stealing her cat was the only remaining option left. I could hear Jamie yell into the ether, "Bailey, I'm summoning up the courage to come get you!"

A year passed, and still I found myself thinking about Jamie. How was she coping? Did she rescue her cat? Where was Bailey living? The only other owner whose story stuck in my head so viscerally was Homeless Mary, but her wretched life was so obviously unforgettable. Jamie's decisions wrenched at me for personal reasons. She was so close. *You're fighting for the one you love!* And without planning to, I called her three times over a period of three years.

The second time we spoke, I found Jamie in a very different state of mind. Several months after our first conversation, she'd walked over to the doctor's house and seen a new face in the window. It belonged to a dog. Intuitively, she knew that Bailey was no longer living there. But she had to be sure. Chancing that no one was home, she jiggled the garage door. It was unlocked. With her heart pounding, she crossed the threshold into the wicked queen's fortress. She sped through every room in the house. She heard meows. Two cats scurried forth from the living room and ran across her feet. Neither was white. Jamie remained silent. The dog barked. She didn't want to make any noise and scare Bailey. But there was no Bailey to scare.

The tears made it hard to see as she closed the garage door.

She walked down the driveway. Her throat tightened and then exploded with sobs. She cried all the way home. Another insight jolted into her consciousness: Bailey had been given to one of their relatives. "I had to release him into the universe," Jamie said. "Bailey was gone forever."

I was sad. Did Jamie pray to the Patron Saint of Lost Causes? I recalled everything that love had propelled her to do. This strong, stubborn woman pissed off an entire neighborhood, endured a year of harassment, held her own with the police, confronted the thief face-to-face, made seven hundred posters, and contacted a chat room, a psychic, and a cat-poster sleuth. But months earlier, when she might have been able to rescue Bailey, something deep inside of her had said no. When she finally entered the criminal's lair, the hostage had been relocated.

"More than anything," the pet detective told me, "I love it when someone calls me up and says that they found their cat or dog. But sometimes my job is a lot of condolences." Bailey's ultimate, incontrovertible disappearance added another layer of sorrow to Jamie's loss—regret. "I had to find a way to deal with me," she said, recalling a fusillade of shoulda-woulda-coulda. "Why didn't I rescue him when I had the chance?" She blamed her general ignorance about the nature of cats as her major failure. Bailey could have been rescued when they first found him on the side of the road. "I wouldn't have scared him."

Loss opened another door on her odyssey. I think the Buddhist farmer left that one unlocked, too. She needed to make amends for losing Bailey. She began donating money to cat causes that advocated Havahart traps and paying out-of-pocket for the spaying of local strays. She and her partner became foster parents, caring for, at their peak, twelve cats at once. Her goals expanded. "I wanted to learn about cats," she explained, "and gain knowledge, so I volunteered at a cat shelter."

"While spending time with the cats," Jamie said, "I started to learn about me. I couldn't understand why Bailey, something

I loved, was taken from me. But I'd hold the cats. They were afraid, at first, of being touched by a stranger, and I could feel the fear in their bodies. I could feel their souls, so to speak. I felt unconditional love for them, and they relaxed, and I began to feel the fear I held in my own body. How it ran my life. Not taking Bailey back when I had the chance. The pain became a gift. Bailey became an inspiration for me to face my own life."

She wasn't at peace, however, when it came to understanding the behavior of the other parties. Why did the police, the animal warden, and the neighbors respond so horribly? Could I tell her why?

"I can make assumptions about their motivation," I told her, "but I think of them more as bit actors in the play about your life, the hero's journey." It's a universal theme—a passage through darkness propelled by a greater or lesser good, or by the subterranean needs of one's own soul. You're torn away from the comfort of what you know and forced to face the darkness in the world. The only way out is to face the darkness in yourself. Spinning your wheels in the mud is an apt metaphor. You can't turn around. There's no possibility of returning to the person you once were. You wish for a rescue, or for fortune to intervene. Going forward is the only way out.

Life doesn't teach us to recognize the modern hero's inner journey. We imagine someone slaying dragons or crossing dimensions, throwing the ring of immortality into an eternal fire, but modern heroes are often threadbare, not cloaked in the king's robes. Our outer landscape has shopping malls, highways, unemployment, marital spats, and oodles of self-destructive options, but facing one's self is timeless—it's the courage to tolerate suffering without knowing why it began or when it will end.

"To come through change not necessarily happier, but wiser and stronger," I told Jamie. "You're the hero."

"I see that people don't always come from trust, or a heart space, or even a logical place," Jamie said. "It hurts to give up that humanistic view." The crack in a good universe had become permanent.

A year later, Jamie and I had our final conversation. Life had resumed without Zak, and I'd returned to my lost-cat poster sleuthing. Unable to reconcile my own recriminations, I returned to what I do best—helping others. By shifting my focus back toward other cat owners, I was hiding, as they say, in plain sight.

And one long, loose thread puckered at the fabric of Jamie's story. I was nagged by her provocative behavior with the neighbors. I couldn't make sense of the contradictions between her actions and her explanations. I wanted to ask her, once again, about her intentions at the time of Bailey's disappearance.

"How do you make sense of your aggressive campaign to get Bailey back?" I asked. "You must have known on some level that you'd antagonize them."

"I was angry with the neighbors," Jamie was able to finally say, and her voice struck a tone that showed she no longer had to split her emotional self from her spiritual self. "I wanted them to fight for Bailey. I was mad at them for not doing what I couldn't do, either."

I understood. The spiritually inclined are often disappointed in the composition of their own feelings because they don't approve of anger, pride, or hate. We want our values to engineer our emotions. But it doesn't work that way. Feelings simply are what they are.

Jamie's life on the outside was no longer familiar. She'd moved to another state. Her relationship had come to an end. She said that losing Bailey had been, in retrospect, the beginning of a series of changes.

I'm speculating, but perhaps losing her cat coincided with an unfathomable truth that took several years to fully illuminate. Maybe her relationship had been quietly unraveling. Maybe her deep intuitive sense of inexplicable sadness had begun mourning something beyond Bailey that couldn't be saved. Something might be coming to a close, but that doesn't mean we want to know it—not yet. Maybe Bailey's loss prepared her for even greater losses to come: love, family, and a changing future. Maybe her experience of helplessness and misdirected anger pulsated to the inevitability about to unfold. Maybe Bailey's loss foreshadowed too much for the psyche to bear all at once.

Jamie loved her new career. The quiet of living in the country helped balance out her hectic schedule. For now, she felt content.

There is a Buddhist parable about a family cat that vanishes.

The client says, "Bad luck now."

A young therapist asks, "How do you feel?"

An older therapist says, "We shall see."

Wie heeft Sam gezien?

Sam is een klein maar stevig katertje met een dik tijgerachtig vachtje en een plat rond koppie en hij woont op de Egelantiersgracht [TEL. 555 5555 OF 555555] struint vaak door de binnentuinen van dit blok. Hij woont hier sinds november en heeft een groenig bandje om met kokertje met naam (en wellicht oude adres er in vermeld). Kijkt u aub even in uw tuinhuis/hok of hij zich daar per ongeluk heeft laten opsluiten.

Wij hopen hem gauw weer terug te zien, dus als u iets weet bel dan aub.

AMSTERDAM
SAM

I flew to Amsterdam to get away from my feelings, and it was working. Then I went for a bike ride and met a man who believed in the future. Not because he could see into it, but because he wanted to love again.

Who Has Seen Sam?

He is thick, tiger-like. Flat round head. Lives on Egelantiers-gracht. He runs thru the yard of this block. He's been living here since Nov. 1 when we moved. He has a green-like collar with a tag with his name on it, but with the old address. Please look in your shed, house, or garden, if he accidentally got locked in.

We hope to see him soon. If you know something, please call us.

"There is no story," he said.

I read the poster again. Even with my marginal understanding of Dutch, it seemed rich with detail, as if every line told a tiny story and hinted at a larger, more cohesive narrative, one that had yet to reach its zenith. I took a longer look at the owner. I couldn't tell if his eyes were blue or gray. Maybe it was that the storyteller didn't want to tell the story. Maybe he wanted to keep it all inside. A hard truth takes time to recognize and accept. Feelings are disorderly. It's what my career is based on.

My holiday in Amsterdam was planned solely for the purpose of escaping a mysterious bout of melancholy. I couldn't pin it on any one source, only that I was having my familiar feelings of restlessness. Nothing I did was truly satisfying. When my friend Anna and her husband asked me to join them on vacation, I was finally excited about something. Karis had recently started a new job, so I went stag.

While we were bicycling through the storybook setting of the Jordan, I discovered a lost-cat poster taped to a window. The Jordan is a neighborhood that looks like the quintessential Amsterdam picture postcard. On each side of the canal is a narrow street running parallel, a skinny bike path, and a brick sidewalk next to a row of stone buildings. Gables cover the rooftops. Trees line the perimeter of the canals, and several hundred houseboats bob in the water.

My mother would have loved this fairy-tale scene. When I was a young traveler she used to say enthusiastically: "Please send me a postcard a day." There were times I'd resented having to find a new postcard. I felt petty. The simple things I didn't want to do for love.

Gray was the color of the day when I saw Sam's poster. Earlier, when the sun had been shining. I had seen several Dutch cat posters, but now the rain was an imperceptible drizzle that left your hands and face covered in a fine mist. It was a day when you tilted your chin down and your bicycle sped faster than the usual tourist crawl. But due to a foreign twist of fate or a crick in the neck—or one too many puddles—I happened to glance to my right. And there I saw a lost-cat poster hanging in the front window of someone's *home*.

The Dutch, while a friendly people, aren't prone to huge displays of feeling. The owners must have been relentlessly bereft. Because most of the residents in Amsterdam are proficient in English, I assumed I wouldn't need an interpreter. I introduced myself at their front door. Tobric responded by tilting his stocky, round head and asking: "Who are you?" He wore a rumpled T-shirt and jeans. He was cautious but polite. They'd been searching for two months, but were still wrestling with their disbelief. How could Sam have broken his routine?

"Sam would only have been able to go in a few directions," Tobric said, pausing mid-sentence as he fished for his English. He was referring to the canals. Because solid ground and landfill were in short supply at the time, the seventeenth-century buildings in Amsterdam stand side by side and are all connected. Therefore, Sam couldn't have snuck into an alley. There are none.

"We know he didn't fall in," he said, looking over my shoulder in the direction of the canal. "Sam's lived next to it his whole life."

Many pets live close to a canal, and approximately two thousand houseboats are permanently occupied and docked in Amsterdam. Cats and dogs have learned to navigate around the canals just as they would the particulars of any environment. One houseboat was particularly intriguing: *Poezenboots,* or "the cat boat," the last of two feline rescue houseboats whose sister had to be taken out of the water for repairs. It appears to be unoccupied unless you look closely and see its furry crew napping on the deck

Tobric considered some other theories. "If he had been hit by a car, we would have known, because Sam had a name tag, and it's a small neighborhood. Someone would know." He rubbed the top of his shaved head.

So far he'd ruled out a car accident, a canal drowning, and an alley escape route. They were sure of one other detail: Sam hadn't disappeared voluntarily. "It's not in his character," Tobric said.

He may have been making a salient point about Sam, but he also could have been referring to the nature of Dutch cats in general. Cats in mellow Amsterdam are more civilized than their American counterparts. They don't try to put their owners through hell. They're too nice. How do I know? The Dutch offer a no-fault disappearance. Amsterdam cats don't run away, escape, bolt, scoot, hide, scamper, skedaddle, or take off like a bat out of hell. *They walk away.* It's a popular expression, used in conversation and in print. ("Sky walked away in the Red Light District." "Bassie walked out on Rogerstien Street." "Tigger walked, too.")

Tobric offered his mix of data and a hypothesis. The garden had secrets. At both his current and former address, Sam had a routine. During the day, he might go out the front entrance or play in the small, enclosed garden near the back of the house. In the evening, he waited by the door until he was let in and remained inside for the night. On the day that Sam disappeared, he'd been playing in the garden. "We came home and Sam was gone," Tobric said. "The next day we had to make posters."

Behind their apartment, a stone wall surrounds the backyard on three sides. The length of the wall separates one street's row of gardens from the other. On the back wall, and almost as tall, are low-hung, shed-like rooftops. Sam could have jumped and run along the wall or the rooftops, but even if he'd bounded into someone else's garden, he couldn't have made it from their garden onto the street unless a neighbor took him inside and opened the front door. The neighbors said they hadn't seen the cat. His options were few. He could jump on the wall, spring into someone else's garden, or go home.

The pattern of Sam's story was familiar. A cat was missing, and no one had a clue. At the same time, I had an odd feeling that compelled me to reiterate that I, too, had turned desperate when my cat vanished. I felt something extra for Tobric. He'd hung Sam's poster in the window of their home. A member of his family was gone.

"Maybe Sam found a hole in the wall," he said. "Even if he did, why wouldn't he crawl back through it? Maybe he's stuck."

He was about to shrug and realized even that was pointless. "It's like losing a child."

There are times with clients of mine when there are no words. Quiet is the therapy. Letting someone breathe and feel without social distractions. I become a witness. The best I can offer at that moment is company. No judgments, suggestions, or insights. Knowing when to shut up counts.

I offered Tobric and his girlfriend my condolences and was about to reach for my bike, when he suddenly said, "We think someone is stealing cats." He looked off into the clouds. "My neighbor told me."

"When did he tell you this?"

"A couple of weeks ago."

"Why?" I asked. "Who would steal a group of cats?"

"We think he steals the cats and sells them," Tobric said. "My neighbor said that in the last two months, five cats and one dog have disappeared. You see, Sam is a British shorthair, and he's worth a lot of money. He's unique."

"Do you think it's more than one person?"

"It's probably a weirdo," he said. "He's a sicko to do this. People know if they find a cat to take it to the authorities. They have a machine. He's got a chip. Our cats are registered, and Sam could be identified, dead or alive. So we think he's stolen. We think the weirdo is keeping him indoors."

In therapy, a client's worst fears are often revealed in the last few minutes of a session. The pressure of a time limit and the knowledge of impending escape encourage a client to voice un-wanted feelings and thoughts and deposit them with me. By proxy, I'll handle it for them. I've often thought that if I shortened my sessions to say, ten minutes, in the ninth minute I'd hear what normally takes a distressed person an hour to reveal. Tobric had finally admitted the unthinkable.

"When I stopped at your door, did you think I was up to no good?"

"We didn't know you," he said, "and you didn't read the poster and walk away. You just stood there."

In Tobric's initial account, "there was no story." But the truth was there were too many. The lost-cat poster told two months' worth of stories. The neighbor told Tobric another. A horror story. Speculation spun on its own axis, but life without Sam was the enduring story.

I looked down at Tobric's feet. One more story was rubbing up against his leg. Sam's brother, Max, had come to visit. His face was shaped like Sam's, only it was a different color. He was a British shorthair, too, but his fur was a shade of silver tinged in sepia and streaked with a whisper of black. The couple had become more protective than they once were. Max couldn't go outside unless one of them was with him, but he was timid, they said, and so far it had been fine.

The act of listening affects the storyteller as much as it does the listener. Confusion, trauma, pain, and shifting thoughts are what begin the tale, but there's a moment when a change occurs in the storyteller's energy. The past loses its omnipotence. The listener senses that the storyteller will be all right.

Tobric looked lovingly at Max and bent down to pet him. Then he spoke, and I heard the future seep in. "We want to get him a brother," he told me. But not just yet. They needed more time.

We said good-bye, then Anna and I took refuge from the rain in a café. I drank a cup of hot chocolate. I felt grateful. I was in wonderful Amsterdam, eating a cheese sandwich and looking out the window at a little bridge stretching over the canal. I didn't want to leave this cozy city. I felt touched by Tobric. He was evaluating his readiness to risk loving again. The five-year-old in me wanted to ask: Where does all the old love that's inside of you go when you can't bear to feel it? I wanted a magician to answer, "Love is never lost."

Maybe all your love goes into a special box with your name on it. When you open the lid it's there, waiting for you.

It seemed that Tobric envisioned a future, one where his sorrow had faded, where he would love again. I was impressed with him. I rarely see uncomplicated grief. Instead of mourning the loss of a loved one, the mourner becomes self-punishing: "It's my fault," "I meant to visit," "Our last words were," or "I should have done more."

I liked the way Tobric was taking care of himself. Loss hadn't become a reason not to love again. Loss needs respect and time to move him—and anyone—out of the past. I wanted to have a touch of Tobric's spirit sprinkled on all of us.

SQUEEZER
IS
LOST!

When the weather is nice he stays on the porch but yesterday afternoon, for some reason, he disappeared. He might be sick.

If you have any information, please stop by our cabin.

Thank you very much.

Ashley and family

SQUEEZER

My plane landed in a fury in New York. I sped home and turned
the key, opening the door to an empty apartment. Karis was at
work. After tossing all of the junk mail, I turned on my computer
and skimmed the titles of my unread e-mails. *Delete. Delete.* "Lost
Cat Story." *What?* I glanced at the sender's address. It was from
my long-lost friend and former teacher Ashley Shelby who had
moved from New York to Minneapolis several years earlier. I'd
recently been thinking about her, but this seemed uncanny. She's
a wonderful writer. I opened the attachment and began reading.

Dear Nancy,

How are you? I hope things are going well out on the East
Coast. I miss it. I have a lost-cat story for you. This time it's mine.
It's been very upsetting to me. In an effort to try to deal with it, I
thought I'd tell you about it. You will understand.

My family has had a cat for nearly twenty years. When I was
thirteen, I received a two-year-old tabby from the pound. She was
instantly my cat. We called her Squeezer. Anyway, after I left for
college, she had to own up to the fact that she was going to have
to deign to be friends with my mom and dad. After a few years,
she and my mother became inseparable. The cat was literally

her best friend. As the cat grew older, she became quirky. She started to chew her fur off. Several trips to the vet and various medications did nothing to alleviate this, and she had no known stressors in her life, besides being forced to watch *So You Think You Can Dance* every Thursday night. When my sixteen-month-old son visited Grandma and Grandpa, Squeezer put up with all the poking and prodding.

I'm fast-forwarding to this past weekend. My mother was in Ithaca helping my sister pack up her house and move into Manhattan and my father went up to our cabin with the dog and the cat. Standard procedure. My dad let Squeezer go outside, as he always did, for a few minutes of fresh air around 4 p.m. on Saturday. After an hour, he got worried. He spent the next two days searching for her, calling her name, to which she always responded. We are surrounded at the cabin by a lake on one side, a house on the other, and a farm across the street.

But my father finally gave up and had to go home to the Twin Cities for work. When my mother returned from Ithaca, she went straight to the cabin and, after another two days of fruitless searching, has come home, heartbroken. Squeezer's so old and feeble I can't imagine her having wandered very far. My mom canvassed the entire west side of the lake and asked people about Squeezer. No one had seen her. She's not at the animal shelter. I posted an ad on Craigslist, but no hits so far.

The thoughts that have been racing through my mind are terrible. Where could she have gone? She was very old—about nineteen years old—but she wasn't showing any signs of a worsening condition. I like to think she knew her time was near and just went off somewhere. To remain undiscovered, to curl up, and pass away. But then I think that maybe she was carried off by something and it makes me physically ill. We don't have any bears around here and no unfriendly dogs. Would a fox do it?

Then the most horrible thought of all is the idea that she

uncharacteristically wandered into the soybean field and got chewed up by one of the farmer's tractors. That would explain why she hasn't been found. I don't actually know if the farmer was out in the fields that weekend, but of course the thought has gone through my mind.

This is really hard, and it gives me even more respect and empathy for the folks you talk to about their lost pets. I don't know how to let this go, because every time I think of her alone in the dark up there, it makes me want to weep.

Anyway, thanks for letting me vent. I hope you and all your loved ones (furry and non-furry alike) are doing well. I am attaching a photo of Squeezer and Hudson, my son, from this past Christmas.

Thanks for listening. All my best.

Ashley

How many ways had she been torturing herself with visions of all of the different ways Squeezer might have met her demise— which included a farm machinery mash-up, a drowning, or being eaten by wild animals? I immediately wrote her back.

Dear Ashley,

I've learned a lot about lost cats, and it starts with the owners. In their attempt to be thorough, all owners conjure the worst scenarios possible and then blame themselves because they didn't use foresight to prevent them from happening. The longer you look, the more the brain imagines and rehearses a future moment of discovery and redemption. To imagine that helplessness will go away is a powerful force in the brain. A pet is a family member, and having a family member wander away and remain missing is gut wrenching. How does one mourn the finality of something that doesn't yet feel final?

Most cats don't travel that far when they are lost. Some

research shows that indoor cats may scoot only a few houses away from their home. Fear takes over their survival instincts. New smells, their own hair, and even their own markings tell them that this new territory is where they belong. It's become their new home. Tragically, they often won't respond to their owner's voice. But, also, they will not respond if they have an internal clock that lets them know they are winding down. Squeezer was nineteen, which is phenomenally old for a cat.

The truth is that as much as we love our cats, we are minimizing the cat part. Their instincts inform them of impending death. When they are old, they go off to die. Alone.

Squeezer didn't get gobbled up by farm equipment or drown, and she didn't get snatched off the porch by an eagle. She changed her habits, as cats are prone to do when they are sick or declining. Not staying by the cabin door was a change. If Squeezer had remained in the house, you would have found her sleeping in some new strange place.

Shock, loss, and guilt flame wild, nightmarish images. Imagining the night and the cold and all of that is *our* response. Cats can see in the dark! We can't. All of my cats, when they wanted to, would stay out in a snowstorm. We can't. We are imagining what we would feel if we lost our family; if we were lost in the woods, at night, feeling frightened and abandoned. The truth is that you miss Squeezer; but she was not helpless and certainly not abandoned. You don't have to punish yourself because you weren't there to protect her from her own biological clock.

Your family related to Squeezer, it seems, as if she were a delicate, high-strung, nervous cat. If so, that created more of a baby feel to her. You guys didn't name her Rocky! It adds to the feeling that you left the "baby" on the porch, and now it's a *CSI* story.

Knock it off. Squeezer was old. She died in the woods and it was okay. It would have been nice if Squeezer could have said,

"I'm going out for a smoke. P.S. Don't wait up." But she's a cat and, instead she followed her nose off the porch. Cry because you had many amazing years with a cat you can no longer hold. Put a picture up and feel how much you love her and always will.

    Much affection,

    Nancy

I hit SEND, unconvinced that I had done enough. Bearing witness can have its limitations. I wanted to be an alchemist. Instead of changing lead into gold, in my world, I'd change frightening thoughts into soothing ones. But I can never anticipate what words will have meaning for someone else. Years after a severe trauma had brought one woman into counseling, she told me why she came back for a second session. "After the first session," she said, "remember what you said to me when I stood in the doorway crying?"

"I wish I had milk and cookies to give you."

"Yeah, it was perfect."

Ashley wrote back the following day. The letter had helped her mom and dad, too. The irony wasn't lost on me. If only my words could talk me out of my darkness, I would be the most successful client I've ever counseled. Two years on and I was still without a cat of my own.

My birthday was the following month and Karis wanted to know, was I interested in planning a party? I went to the bookshelf and pulled out old photo albums. I looked back at some of my finest celebrations. At least half of the attendees had been acquaintances, neighbors, and colleagues, the casual guests drifting in and out my life. The people that mattered most to me, the ones I loved, were often absent from the photographs. We lived far away from each other.

I wanted something lasting. I wanted to travel somewhere new. Create experiences that would inspire me for the rest of my life. Where to go? I walked into the bathroom and stood a foot back from our shower curtain. It was an ocean blue vinyl map of the world. Continents and countries added their own shiny colors. Let's see: affordability, time, and language factored in. Sunny counted. It didn't take me long to decide. I glided over to my computer and began typing: *international flights*.

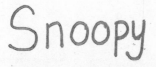

Snoopy

Me llamo Snoopy. Soy muy manso, tengo buen carácter i me llevo bien con otros animales.
Mi pelaje es de un bonito color rubio i tengo unos expresivos ojos verdes.
Tengo diez años y como ya no soy un bebé respetaré todas tus cosas.
Estoy triste porque me he quedado sólo y me gustaría estar contigo para hacerte compañía.

SPANISH SNOOPY

An hour's train ride from Barcelona, a small medieval town sits on a hill overlooking the Mediterranean. Sitges's gentle slope tilts the narrow, winding streets and thimble-sized shops toward the sea. The sky was overpoweringly blue the day I arrived, and, lively conversations in Spanish, German, French, and Italian alternated in the air. I lingered at a small table in an open-air café, under a sun so hot that the houses on the southern slope, most of which were painted white, had their windows shuttered against the midday heat. I took a sip of lemon water and gazed up the hill.

My mother would have loved it here. She'd always wanted a house at the beach. After much contemplation, I picked out her make-believe summer home and then ordered some tapas.

Snoopy's lost-cat poster rested on the table. Early that morning, I saw the poster taped inside a tiny grocery store, but after pushing on the door it wouldn't budge. Taking a step back, I saw a second sign in Spanish stating that the store was closed until Monday. But Monday was four days away and I'd be back in New York. This was my only poster sighting in Spain. I held up my camera phone and pretended to be a photojournalist shooting under rugged conditions. Perhaps I could blow up the fine print.

A few blocks down the road, I spied a second poster of Snoopy in a pet store window. In my best high school Spanish, I asked the clerk if I could copy *"el photo."* She thought that Snoopy was my cat.

"No," I tried to clarify. *"Snoopy no es mi gato. Quiero el photo, un copy."* My Spanish was passable, but the clerk was frightened. There was no precedent for my request. She had to ask her manager. Could I come back tomorrow?

The abundance of text on the poster gave me an idea. Snoopy's owners appeared to be detail-oriented, which I took to mean that they were thorough, too. They must have put up posters in other locations. I asked a man on the sidewalk for directions to a *"medico por gatos y perros."* He pointed and said, *"Derecha"* (to the right).

In the vet's waiting room, Snoopy's poster and two others were hanging on the bulletin board. There were extra copies behind each of them. One poster read, *"Se Busca"* (Searching). Another read, *"Perdido"* (Lost). I took a copy of *"Se Busca."*

I smiled at the photograph of tender-looking Spanish Snoopy. He was wide-eyed and eager to play. Involuntarily I felt an affinity for him—he was orange, like Zak, but smaller. I decided to give Snoopy's family a call. It was only a matter of time until I figured out the local phone system.

I met Karis on the beach and sat down next to her, on a royal blue chaise lounge under a matching umbrella. Karis was absorbed in her book, so I opened my Spanish dictionary and began the task of translating Snoopy's story. The poster read: "My name is Snoopy. I am easygoing. I am good and get along well with other animals. I am a pretty red color. I have green eyes. I am ten years old."

Not so rusty, I thought with a newfound confidence. By the water's edge, teenage boys kicked a soccer ball and grandmothers sunbathed topless. This is the life I was meant to live—a beautiful ocean view, a fabulous hotel, and room service. Everyone, even therapists, have a fantasy of leaving their known and routine life behind for something more exotic. What would it take to start over?

How do you run away to a foreign country? Should I take up smoking? Everyone else in Spain had. I'd have to leave my career behind, close down my practice. I mentally composed a termination letter to my clients. Sensitivity was the key.

Dear 9 a.m.,

In this crazy, mixed-up world, you don't always get what you want, but you can get what you need. Your therapist needs to live at the beach in Costa del Sol. Moving to Europe precludes my availability to offer you ongoing psychotherapy.

The doctors have assured me that my lifespan would increase by decades simply by living in a hotel overlooking the ocean, particularly if the room service is excellent. Lamb chops should be consumed every Sunday. As you know, doctors rarely give such specific recommendations.

If life on the Mediterranean is meant to be, I can't fight destiny. I am only its humble servant, and according to my astrologer, an upcoming change of scenery is in the works. Jupiter and Mars will soon be in my ninth house of travel.

Of course, your welfare is of the utmost importance to me. This is why I carefully reviewed your records. In my professional opinion, you should continue in therapy. Just not with me. After you were indicted for insider trading and leveraged your McMansion, I became very concerned about your financial fragility and the need to live within your own means. Sorry your stock options are worth bupkis. It's a new world order, but I find change refreshing. So will you.

I just wanted to give you a heads-up.

Dr. Nancy

P.S. I'll bring coffee and the good-bye cake.

Not too shabby for a first draft, but translating Snoopy's poster took priority for the rest of the afternoon. The vocabulary was increasingly challenging, and my pocket dictionary was limited. Still, I got the gist of it. Snoopy had swallowing and respiratory problems. Now I was worried. Snoopy was sick and missing.

I needed to stretch, so I took a walk. On my way back, I saw an orange cat sitting on a ground-floor terrace. He meowed at me. Like Snoopy, he reminded me of Zak. He was warm and friendly and he rubbed up against my legs. For a brief moment, I hesitated, and then I put my hand out and stroked his chin. I met his owners, an expatriate American couple who'd been living in Sitges for twenty years. They were living my European dream. I showed them my lost-cat poster—maybe they could help me find Snoopy's owner, or at least help me to understand his illness.

"What's wrong with Snoopy?" I asked.

The wife took the poster and they both read it in silence. Afterward, they glanced at each other and smiled. I wasn't smiling. Next, they took turns reading one sentence in Spanish and then translating it into English. I thought I'd done a respectable job of it, until she said, "Snoopy will not touch your things."

"What does that have to do with being lost?" I asked, though I was used to owners providing esoteric descriptions. The couple laughed at me, but they held back the big guffaw. "He will make a good companion for others."

Why would a lost cat need a companion? Then it dawned on me. Snoopy's *not* lost. He isn't sick, and he isn't missing. The owner was trying to find a loving home for Snoopy. I'd made up a lost-cat poster.

I looked lamely at the couple, and then mustered a smile. We chatted for a bit and then I straggled back to the beach. I wanted to diagnose myself. Getting a C in Spanish was a contributing factor. *"Se Busca"* had tricked me—Snoopy was grouped with the other missing cats. *Hallucination?* Not really. Snoopy was a cat, and all I saw was a cat on a poster. *Wake-up call* was probably more accurate. It was time to stop collecting posters for good.

When I reached my umbrella, I put my towel down on the sand and looked at Karis, gripping *The Lord of the Rings* with both hands. She was lost in Middle Earth. I slid down onto my back and stared off into the sky. Why was I still collecting posters? My original questions, the ones that had spurred my quest, had been answered long ago.

Do lost-cat posters facilitate a cat's return? The answer was a qualified yes.

Had other cat owners received empathic phone calls from strangers? Half of the people I talked to said yes.

While in the midst of a frantic search, did owners of missing cats take the time to laugh at themselves? In my skewed study, I'd say the majority had moments of both humor and dread.

Do personality and temperament affect the nature of a cat owner's search? Clearly.

How many missing cats return without assistance? At least a third.

What makes a happy ending? Only the owner can decide. You can find your cat and lose your faith in people, or you can lose your cat and find your faith.

It was time to stop, but snooping for cat posters had become second nature to me. Smokers get a nicotine patch. Alcoholics go to meetings. I needed a patch and a meeting.

I also needed a nap. I put on my sunglasses and fell asleep.

When I woke up, I looked out at the ocean. After seven years of searching for lost-cat posters, it seemed time to give up the journey, although I felt reluctant to do so. A memory came into focus. As a child, I would pick one wave in the ocean and follow its gleaming arc in order to find that exquisite moment after it crashed and rolled onto the sand, when there was neither ebb nor flow. I didn't yet know the word "elusive," but I knew the feeling. I felt it now. I was between two worlds, the past and the future.

I walked to the water's edge and looked at the ocean's mellowing tide. Birds wet their feet in low puddles of seawater. In the background, the rays of the setting sun cast their sweeping columns of light toward the beach, while waves wrinkled at the water's edge. I could feel the heat of the day and a soft night wind coming closer. I felt my connection to a great life force.

I thought about the tremendous momentum and ambition this life force has given me, and the obstacles, as well. I wanted many experiences, and I sought them out through travel, relationships, adventures, studies, sports, philosophies, religions, and people. When I was young, I didn't understand why I became so sad when a particular experience was over. After all, I loved novelty and change. Why couldn't I move on? I would leave the last page of a book unturned, because I wasn't ready to let the experience go.

In my twenties, while reading a travel magazine during a flight home from Paris, I was introduced to the French phrase *melancholy de voyage,* "the sadness of travel." I felt less lonely upon realizing that part of my reaction was universal. We will never meet again in the same way. Change and loss are inevitable. Change causes suffering in everyone. And although I imagined that I would feel my grief as intensely as before, I thought I could be kinder toward myself in the process.

The realization of the universality of loss also helped to push aside my sense of societal alienation, which had been burned into my youthful heart while I sat on the library floor sobbing. At last, my humanity opened the door to commonality. I was much more than a humiliated, stigmatized identity. I was a traveler in life, like everyone else.

"I know you blame yourself for Zak's death," I heard Karis say as she approached me from behind. Snoopy's poster was in her hand. I felt a chill. I could feel her green eyes on me. But it was time. I felt a sad relief while sinking my feet into the sand. Saying out loud to her what had been suppressed inside. Shuttling back and forth to New York, I'd allowed him to become inconvenient. Maybe he sensed it. I left him alone in the days leading up to his death. I didn't protect him. The ghost of the girl I had believed myself to be hadn't loved Zak well.

"Listen to me," Karis said, her eyes determined, though the edge of a smile was gathering force, too. "It's been a long time. Even Zaky has forgiven you." My eyes watered. It was the perfect thing to say because it was true. Zak *had* forgiven me. A long time ago.

In the days that followed I thought about my undercurrent of loss and self-blame. I so easily embrace them. But I also remembered the girl who identified with the phoenix rising and how she learned to resurrect from loss, change, and pain. My career—really my life's calling—has allowed me to understand resilience, and how to help others create more resilience within themselves. That's how I see my job. I'm teaching clients how to endure what seems unendurable, and to flourish despite loss. Although love itself is part of the cycle of losing and finding, life is a series of comings and goings, and in between we try to cherish and hold on to what we love.

Much of our grief and longing can be traced back to the desire not to feel inadequate and the deep regret we feel at not having mastered life before we have to live it. I don't understand why we suffer so, but I do understand what we can do about it. You find in life, a way to appreciate less, when you were sure you needed so much more. In the face of adversity, you can draw upon most anything to persevere: intelligence, character, honor, compassion, faith, dreams, intuition, imagination, humor, memories, and animals, too.

Some years ago, a new client recovering from an abusive childhood sat on the couch and slapped her own face when she felt inarticulate. "No more hitting," I told her, and she stopped, but she remained silent, eyes dull and lost. After several minutes, I decided casual conversation was best. "Do you have any pets?"

Marcia smiled. "Two cats."

"What are their names?"

"Stable and Journey," she said. My eyes watered, and I felt a seismic shift in her prognosis. Stable was her quest in life and therapy would be the journey, and she knew it. Four years later, Marcia was stable and flourishing. She'd adopted a third cat.

"What's his name?"

"Shalom."

I chuckled. It's Hebrew, but she wasn't Jewish. *Shalom* means "peace and good-bye." Our journey was officially over.

Many people have asked me: "How can you listen to people's problems?" My mother wanted to know: "Is it depressing?" When people learn that I collect lost and found cat stories, I hear a similar question: "Isn't that depressing?"

No, not to me. I'm intrigued by how people manage to navigate the tricky terrain of their lives. I find it exciting. I like hearing how resourceful people can be. I admire inventiveness and determination. Those are important aspects of the journey. But resilience involves more than courage and ingenuity. Sometimes one's capacity to endure suffering includes railing against having to feel it. Sometimes people remain stuck for a long time. Angry, too. I feel compassion when my clients wrestle with their demons. I'm interested in how people create solutions for the problems that life poses for them.

Searching for a lost cat is based on improvisation. A crisis compels us into the unknown. I'm touched by what people are willing to do out of love for their pets. I'm equally touched by the grace exhibited when a pet remains missing. I love stories of resilience, and while I prefer that owners find their pets, I still want to speak with them, even if they're grieving. I love belonging to the subculture of cat owners. I feel less alone. And even if

I become melancholy because of the endings in my own life, I won't become melancholy because of someone else's pain. I want to help them.

I thought about what I'd learned from the cat posters, and like most seekers who embark on a quest, I realized that I'd changed. I no longer saw the world as I had before. Lost-cat posters had taken on a metaphorical meaning for me. They became reminders of impermanence and how we must learn to cope with the inevitability of change. Love can't protect us from time itself. Finally I understood more than the emotional significance of Holly's story about Eccles. Her story embodied the live-action version of the cycle of lost and found, which is life itself. "Lost and found" as a theme permeates almost everything we consider to be meaningful in life. I'd become acutely aware of words and how we use them to describe matters of importance. Our very language says it all.

"I *lost* my confidence." "*Lost* my self-respect." "*Lost* my health, job, and house." "*Lost* my life savings." "*Lost* my kids." "*Lost* my virginity." "*Lost* my sobriety." "*Lost* sight of what's important." "*Lost* my mind." "*Lost* my best friend/mother/brother/husband to cancer." "Life *lost* all meaning." "I *lost* weight." "*Lost* interest." "*Lost* my faith." "*Lost* my home." "*Lost* my way." "I *lost* a reason to live." "I *lost* my will, wallet, and keys." "*Lost* my cat, too."

"But I *found* myself." "*Found* my voice." "*Found* God." "*Found* peace." "*Found* my heart and soul." "Finally *found* the nerve." "I'm *finding* out how to love myself." "*Found* the love of my life." "*Found* the truth." "*Found* my life's calling." "*Found* my identity." "*Found* a community." "*Found* forgiveness." "Finally *found* what I've been looking for." "I *found* the courage." "I *found* my passion." "I *found* my cat."

And my favorite:

"*I found my way. Again.*"

Zak, the cat that started it all.

ACKNOWLEDGMENTS

One of the kindest people I know is the author, editor, and teacher, Ashley Shelby Benites. When there was scant evidence to do so, she believed in me and selflessly guided me through the process of becoming an author. Without her support, experience, and triage skills I would not have completed this book.

I celebrate all the authors who encouraged me especially during the early stages of this project; thank you Jack Hitt, Professor Tony Rosso, my prolific brother, Jeff Davidson, and the Train Lady aka Joanna Baymiller.

I feel blessed to have had so much support. Karis Wold, thank you for your sly wit and artistic style.

In New Haven, I am thankful to my buddies for their years of support, including Sunday supper with Rosemary Coratola and Judith Honorowski. Thank you Marilyn Acquarulo, Lulu's Café, Peter Peter, Jill Fluffy Zamparo, and Faith Middleton.

In New York, I am extremely grateful to my agent Stephen Barr from Writers House. He rescued my manuscript from the slush pile and gambled on it. He was a patient but driving force in making my unpolished manuscript shine. I am in his debt. I also deeply thank Brenda Copeland, my editor at St. Martin's Press for her vision, commitment, experience, sense of humor, and the contribution of her beloved cats Edna and Bruiser. Thank you Laura Chasen for being a steady bright light. And kudos to the art department! I thank the very loving Elizabeth Carl for her years of creative guidance and constant enthusiasm. Much appreciation goes to Katelyn Lovejoy for her editorial feedback.

In Los Angeles, I thank from the bottom of my heart my generous and outstanding friend from the third grade, Jamie L. Smith, who is always wise in the ways of the world. I thank her swimming pool. West Coast kitty too.

My gratitude to the source of life itself and our endless opportunities for second chances.

RESOURCES

VOLUNTEER! ADVOCATE! DONATE!

TAKE SOMEONE FURRY HOME!

The Humane Society of the United States (http://www.humane society.org). The Humane Society of the United States (HSUS), has a membership of more than 7 million. It is the nation's largest animal organization committed to using legal, educational, legislative, and investigative means to protect animals.

The American Society for the Prevention of Cruelty to Animals (ASPCA) (http://www.aspca.org). The ASPCA was the first humane organization in the Western Hemisphere. The ASPCA works to rescue animals from abuse, pass humane laws, and share resources with shelters nationwide.

The American Humane Association (http://www.americanhu mane.org). The mission of American Humane Association uniquely combines ensuring the welfare, wellness, and well-being of children and animals. It offers a range of programs to further our connections between humans and animals.

ADOPTION, NON-PROFIT

Petfinder.com is an online, searchable database of animals need-ing homes. It is also a directory of more than 13,000 animal shelters and adoption organizations across the United States, Canada, and Mexico. Organizations maintain their own home pages and available-pet databases. Petfinder is made up of animal-care professionals and regular people who volunteer.

TRAP-NEUTER-RETURN FOR FERAL CATS

Alley Cat Allies (www.alleycat.org). Alley Cat Allies wants to stop the estimated 70 percent kill rate that occurs in animal shelters. They developed a Trap-Neuter-Return model for low-ering the reproduction rates of feral cats. They offer ground-breaking advocacy and hands-on education for cat devotees including humane trapping, feral cat colony care, and forming public policy.

LOW-COST SPAY DIRECTORY USA

Love that cat.com (http://www.lovethatcat.com/spayneuter .html). This site gives important information about neutering for pet owners. It offers a long list, by state, of programs provid-ing low cost or free spay/neuter for cats.

WHAT TO DO
WHEN YOUR CAT GOES MISSING

1. **Look in new and old places.** Start inside your home. Cats have a habit of stowing away in their homes, so check odd spots and nooks and crannies. Felines love to hide under furniture (especially beds), in closets, boxes, or high on top of shelves. More than one cat has been found in the dryer and even within a recliner chair.

2. **Leave food in random places in and out of doors.** Often a missing cat will mysteriously reappear when lured by his favorite treat.

3. **Scour the neighborhood.** Cats are territorial and chances are that your cat is nearby. They find safe spots, such as tool sheds or garages, when they are out of their normal environments. Again, look for likely hiding places: under cars, under porches and bushes. Bring a flashlight. Bring treats and shake the container to get your cat's attention.

4. **Ask friends and neighbors to help you look.** Searching for a lost cat can be lonely work. You'll be glad of the company—and the extra pair of eyes—even if it's only for half an hour.

5. Call your cat by name. Keep your voice encouraging. You may be frightened, but your cat is also. Stay upbeat.

6. Create at least *fifty* lost-cat posters.
- Use bright colors and photographs.
- If you can't use color photographs, use colored paper.
- Focus on your cat's face. Use a close-up photo.
- Use a strong headline. Instead of the generic "Lost Cat," go for something like MISSING TABBY or LOST CALICO or CHESTER IS LOST.
- Select a bold font that can be seen by passing cars.
- Position posters so that they face oncoming traffic.
- Be detailed. Include your cat's name, as well as the time and place he was last seen. Include the date!
- Don't forget the contact information. A cell phone number is best.
- Attach posters to telephone poles in the immediate neighborhood, especially intersections where cars may be stopped while waiting for the lights to change.
- Put up flyers at the bulletin board at the supermarket, library, and community center.
- Leave posters in your neighbors' mailboxes.
- Place posters in shelters, veterinary offices, pet stores, and other places where someone who has found a missing cat may think to look.
- Use social media: Twitter and Facebook can reach hundreds, even thousands, of people.

7. Widen your search. If you haven't found your cat after twenty-four hours of looking, extend your area of searching.

8. Contact your police department in case anyone has reported finding a lost cat.

9. **Place an advertisement in your local paper** and check the "Lost Pets" section.

10. **Go to your local animal shelter—repeatedly.**
    - You may not receive accurate information over the phone. Go in person. You may think of Baxter as a "cuddly tuxedo cat," but the staff may see him as a "chubby black & white."
    - New pets come in all of the time, and the staff changes several times a day. Visit your local shelter frequently, at least every other day.
    - Leave a lost-cat poster with the shelter attendants when you visit.
    - Ask about recently deceased cats. It may be hard to hear, but it's better to know than wonder.
    - Check all shelters within fifty miles of where your cat went missing. Your cat may have strayed farther than you think.

11. **FOLLOW YOUR INTUITION!**

WHAT TO DO
WHEN YOU FIND A CAT

1. If you've found a cat that you think is lost, first place at least a dozen "Found" posters in the immediate vicinity. The more eye-catching, the better.

2. Check and recheck with your neighbors to see if anyone has lost a cat.

3. Ask the police department. Someone may have reported a missing cat. Be sure to give a detailed physical description.

4. Many pet owners now outfit their animals with microchip tracking devices. Take the cat to a veterinary clinic to see if he has a tracking device.

5. Drop off posters at veterinary offices, pet stores, shelters, and other places where an owner may look.

6. Check online sites in your area; the sites may vary but you can begin with a generic title: lost and found pets.

7. Contact local rescue/animal shelter groups and give them a detailed description of the cat.

8. Place a "Found Pet" ad in your local newspaper. Please leave out certain identifying information. If anyone calls claiming to be the cat's owner, feel free to immediately ask each person to describe his or her cat.

9. Never volunteer information or answer questions. The caller should provide details about the cat or where and when the cat disappeared. Scam artists often fish for information.